How to Analyze People

Learn Speed Reading Others' Body Language. Spot if a Narcissist Manipulates You and Defend Yourself from Dark Psychology, Mind Control, Deception, Gaslighting, NLP & Persuasion

BLAKE CODE

© Copyright 2019 - All rights reserved.

HOW TO ANALYZE PEOPLE

First edition. October 2019.

Copyright © 2019 Blake Code.

Written by Blake Code.

Table of Contents

Introduction

Congratulations for purchasing *How to Analyze People,* and thank you for doing so. Mind manipulations have been on the rise since the 1800s with the practice lacking awareness at the time. Today, multiple groups involve the art of mind control while focusing solely on influencing thoughts and behaviors of the victim. As such, the victims remain in an unknown state of mind but insisting that he or she participates in certain activities willingly.

The book *How to Analyze People* highlights the general information available concerning mental manipulation, including tracing back research done under the topic. With mind-control becoming rampant in our culture today, technology and seeking immediate solutions to existing problems play a significant role in enhancing mind control techniques among individuals. The art of mind control can be used either positively or negatively depending on the manipulator. The positive mind controls improve life by enabling us to focus on what we want to achieve.

On the other hand, negative mind control techniques may lead to cults, victims involving in chaotic behaviors and sometimes death. Manipulators should, therefore, focus on bringing the food out of it rather than influencing others negatively. Besides, the art of mind control may involve a self-drive or manipulation from other individuals. Self-drive mind control techniques enable you to clear your mind and feel the emptiness, therefore, focusing on what is essential. Mind control from secondary sources is frequently negative, destroying the lives of their victims.

There are plenty of books on this subject on the market, thanks again for choosing this one! Every effort was made to ensure it is full of as much useful information as possible. Please enjoy!

CHAPTER 1:
The Art of Mind Control

With the digital world quietly settling around us, machines are the forefront in satisfying our hunger for more advanced technologies in our societies. About three decades ago, the art of mind control seemed like a cult and confined to specific cultures. Similarly, many saw mind control as an impact of mental disorders affecting certain people. For instance, when given a ten thousand puzzle to solve within an hour or two, your mind will initially ask questions such as 'why?' and 'how will it benefit you at the end.' The mind primarily never likes failing henceforth; you remain in a constant act of thinking new things or solving different emerging challenges.

History of Mind Control

The art of mind control comprises of some science behind it originating in the 1980s by researcher Dr. Robert Cialdini. In a book entitled Influence: The Psychology of Persuasion, Dr. Robert highlights crucial principles proven to influence individuals. Mind control has therefore been proven scientifically and not generalized as magic, arcane arts, or mental problems. Between 1800 and 1810, James Tilly Matthews drew the first technical drawing prototypes which led to significant confusions between people. With minimal knowledge about the art of mind control at the time, his picture brought a lot of controversy among the population as they never understood its meaning.

As such, Mathews was locked up in the Royal Bethlem Hospital and considered a lunatic but claimed to be detained illegally. The authority at the time insisted that his drawings suggested a different action. However, Mathews explained about his pictures, which comprised of a completely different message difficult for other people to understand. Recently, pioneer Rod Dickinson translated Mathew's hallucinatory drawings into reality, bringing out a more comprehensive and modern picture never witnessed before.

Over the years, the art of mind control has loomed globally with different individuals equipped with the skills of controlling minds. Like Mathews, Maverick and Victor Tausk also developed a complex framework in 1919 inspired by Natalija. She was held against her will after her thoughts on dreams being influenced by electronics devices run by a faction of doctors in Germany. The last few centuries have experienced increased visions across our cultures and amplified but influenced by those whom it originated with.

What Is Mind Control?

Mind control is the act of manipulation, mental power, and brainwashing, coercive persuasion, and thought reformation leading to an individual to get disrupted and lose their own authority. With so many titles used to describe mind control, some groups may decide on one definition depending on how they view the thoughts of oneself. For example, addicts may utilize the art of mind control for their benefits but with inherently wrong situations. On the other hand, groups which practice one on one cults benefit on the weakness of their target persons and manipulate their minds abusively.

With a definition provided by psychologist Philip Zimbardo, the art of mind control entails a situation where freedom of choice of an individual or a given population is compromised. The manipulation therefore modifies or distorts perception, behavior, and cognition, among others, and everyone is susceptible to such agents or agencies. The ancient generation describes mind control as an act of a manipulator to combine words and pressures of people, creating dependency and influence their thoughts. The persons being controlled are unaware of either their actions or changes.

Mind Control Vs. Brainwashing

According to Steve Hassan, there exists a difference between mind control and brainwashing, especially when the manipulation remains on two separate individuals. Steve states that brainwashed victims understand that their manipulators are their enemy as well as they intend no good in the end. For instance, brainwashed soldiers realize who the enemy is and systems to adapt to remain alive. The influence of brainwashing also disappears over time with individuals becoming healthy again.

Mental control, on the other hand, involves subtle and insidious processes with the manipulator being more of a friend, teacher, or known to you. The victim is thus remaining conversant with the procedure of mind control. The art under subtle entails an individual being aware of the extent of the influence; therefore, the need to make necessary changes over time. Mind control becomes insidious when the victim lacks a move to make decisions of themselves but the manipulators making choices for them.

Susceptibility

Every individual around the world is vulnerable to the art of mind control despite some research stating that the weak being the most susceptible. Cults are among the leading groups continuously recruiting a new member and doing what is necessary to keep them. However, some remain positive that such cases are a myth and never vulnerable to be mind-controlled. Such people are the most susceptible as they are not on the lookout and avoid situations leading to mind control.

To protect yourself, you must learn about such topics in-depth henceforth guaranteeing safety against involving in mind control activities while unaware. The current world has also created more room for people to be susceptible to mind-controlling events. For instance, cults offer solutions to practical problems such as safety and order, enabling more people to get recruited through the art of mind control. The same applies to films released today about mind control, which again attract individuals to try and involve in mental manipulation.

Factors Affecting the Art of Mind Control

- Skills of mind manipulators
- Techniques used
- Extend of techniques involved

- Frequency of exposure of the victim to mind control
- Methods utilized in the process, either hypnosis or hypnotic

Signs Someone Is Using Mind Control against You

Isolation

Mind control primarily affected your behavior and thoughts; therefore, you may become unaware of any practice you undertake. The same applies to isolate yourself from your family and friends without your knowledge. When you begin being by yourself, especially from your loved ones, then it is a sign of mind control. Your manipulators focus on your loneliness and vulnerability as well as providing new friends aware and reluctant when your spirit is being to apart.

Immediate Change of Behavior

There are situations where you have similar habits overtime either with your partner or friends. However, there are instances where you begin to change your behavior, especially when facing a challenge. Your partner or friends may notice these, but you may remain in the dark while your manipulators succeed in controlling your mind. Becoming moody and sometimes too good to your loved one is a sign that someone is succeeding in manipulating your mind and gaining control over your thoughts.

Metacommunication

When you, your partner or friend begin communicating in nonverbal cues through subtle and hints, then it becomes a sign of mind control. For instance, when you ask your partner if he or she is fine, and the reply is positive with a sigh and shrug; then the answer becomes obvious that mind-controlling activities are happening. More so, some may utilize metacommunication to suggest their solutions to bring out subliminal thoughts. When you or your partner experiences such, you are under control of someone else's charm.

Uncompromising Regulations

Do you experience harsh and unreasonable rules at your house from your partner or strict regulations on certain activities? This is a type of mind control to take over your decisions to follow another set of behavior. Strict regulations, therefore, halt your thinking while suppressing over your lifestyle as well as your time. Uncompromising rules make you weak and vulnerable for your manipulators to readily implant their agendas in your mind.

Effect of Neuro-Linguistic Programming

Neuro-linguistic programming involves implanting influential thoughts while utilizing an individual's unconscious mind without their knowledge to perform certain activities. The mode used depends on the aspect of mind control of the victim, therefore, using manipulated languages to deliver fake suggestions. For example, blind people will be addressed in the form of 'Can you *see* what is meant?' For such cases, your mind is under control, and your manipulator may be up to no good.

Preventing the Art of Mind Control from Secondary Sources

As mentioned earlier, everyone is susceptible to mind control, and escaping a manipulator may also become more complicated. If you notice signs and feel like you are being controlled; escaping involves doing the opposite of what is intended. Visit your loved ones who include friends and family members and avoiding those who prevent you from seeing them. Another form is avoiding sulky behaviors by maintaining your usual character and solving problems as required. Avoid nonverbal cues during conversations.

Impacts of neuro-Linguistic programming are one of the most difficult to spot as individuals who use them are professionals. As such, ensure you remain vigilant on people who mirror your body languages as well as use meaningless vague phrases. For those imposing uncompromising regulations, seek professional advice or from friends as reduced self-esteem encourages mind control activities. Reaction from your family, friends, or psychiatrist would provide you with adequate guidelines on what is transpiring in your thoughts.

Essential Mind Control Techniques

Our minds are the most potent elements but can only be controlled using different mind control techniques. Positive techniques encourage a good life with a unique aspect occurring on contrary objectives leading to lack of control of your thoughts. Essential mind control techniques include implanting a given idea in mind and creating a feeling of emotion desirable for training your brain. Our minds understand the source of your happiness, as such; our subconscious thoughts control emotions, life outlook, and attitudes, among others.

Visualization Technique

Visualizing about our lives are crucial mind control procedures enabling us to work towards achieving success. Positive visualizations attract significant accomplishments in life; for example, sports psychiatrists utilize these mind control methods to enhance performance in athletics. For a good experience with the art of mind control, visualization prepares us to face newer and unexpected challenges that life brings. Your feelings are thus enhanced with a perceived well-being nature drawn from the immediate environment.

Manifesting Positives Visualization Technique

Creative Visualization

Creative visualization enables you to create an image in your mind of what you want and helps you to focus on achieving it. This method requires strong intent and emotions until you visualize its success in your mind. The feeling should also run within your body, accompanied by emotions both made possible by the law of nature. Creative visualization aligns your thoughts with the energy of the universe.

Positive Assertion

There are thought of statements and declarations you make firmly several times a day, eventually creating a strong feeling in your mind. These words develop in your subconscious mind, which actives the converting those thoughts into reality and positive energy. Positive assertions, therefore, enables your brain to focus on what you want. Similarly, the technique creating intense energy, making you aware of what you want to achieve as your goals.

Other Forms

Other manifestations of visualization technique of mind control are getting rid of fear and negative thoughts, letting go of stressful thinking and creating positive attitudes. You may also medicate through silence and focusing solely on your objectives, and being thankful are vital components. Besides, spend time with motivated and successful people filled with happiness and hope who spread their feelings with you.

Meditation Technique

Meditation technique began long ago hence one of the oldest methods used in the art of mind control. The technique involves calming the mind and emptying all your thoughts allowing peace to overflow your mind. With the calmness and emptiness of the brain, your subconscious takes control, and you can hear your mind quietly. During the meditation period, the mind releases alpha waves, which are proven scientifically to aid in learning the peak of the process. Alpha waves provide room for your mind to be filled with positive thoughts and enrich them with creative thinking. You remain empowered and concentrate on the present while forgetting the past, thus focusing on crucial elements of your life.

Mirror Talk Technique

Mirror talk technique may sound crazy to most users but essential helping your think straight and achieve the best with your life. The mirror is the best friend and worst enemy to man. It primarily depends on how you encourage yourself while in front of the mirror. Mirror talk technique entails facing yourself through the mirror and has a self-conversation about the present and the future. Negative talks deteriorate our self-esteem, and when you walk, you feel looked upon by everyone you meet. One the other hand, positive discussions enables you to increase your self-confidence. Positive strokes enhance our courage allowing us to focus on what is necessary, therefore engaging in available activities.

Self-Hypnosis Technique

Like meditation, self-hypnosis also focuses on emptying your mind and focus on your subconscious voice on what you need the most. This technique is the most used, especially for alcoholics with a total dependency on alcohol and creating a new life for themselves free from substances. Combination of self-hypnosis and repetition on a single mantra provides a beneficial outcome as many may suffer most rampant and sophisticated complications.

Focusing on Goals and Self-Assessment

As a good life art of mind control technique, highlighting your goals and assessing yourself continuously significant assist in relaxing your mind and create essential thoughts. The goals should be concrete and focus on what you want to achieve. You should also review your goals frequently to avoid working outside your restrictions. Change what is necessary and review each progress keenly to keep your purpose on the track and main ting your spirit.

Setting Up Your Life Goals

Setting up your target objectives as a technique of mind control requires selecting those with available capabilities and within your boundaries. Before setting up your mind, and follow your goals, ensure you have full control of your thoughts while working towards your dream. Goals give your directions and guide you through the resources needed, time, and effort to produce meaningful results. Goals also enable you to see all the opportunities and capitalize on them and never miss the essential ones.

Long-Term Goals Vs. Short Time Goals

Long-term goals are those who take a longer time to achieve and sometimes may demand endurance and patience. For instance, you may choose to buy a house in two years. As such, you require a lot of effort to acquire the amount needed and extra work on how you plan to maintain the home. Short-term goals are achieved within a short time, for instance, a day, week, or month and may demand less endurance compared to long-term goals. When considering short-term goals, ensure your plan is set according to your need as late modifications may result in failures or delivery of unworthy outcome.

Subsequently, many individuals face a challenge to decide which plan to select between long-term and short-term goals. Long-term goals are more complicated hence vital for you to break down the list for more natural and straightforward involvements. Break some of the long-term goals to short-term ones and achievements of short time targets prepare you to face long-term goals mentally.

The Art of Mind Control in Technology

Advancement of technology has expanded into mind control with people being able to control objects and games with their minds. From movies to reality, experts managed to design devices translating human brain waves as commands to perform a specific function. Mind-controlled technologies utilize a brain-machine interface to create a pathway of interaction between the user and an external gadget. The same applies to EEG sensors used in games; hence, a player readily controls the game with a headset. EEG uses exoskeletons to translate brain signals essential for users to control bionics through implanted electrodes.

Researchers used a similar practice of mind control in the 1920s to discover human brain electrical activities henceforth creating electroencephalography to record the events in the scalp. In 1969, the first experiment, done by Eberhard Fetz, involved a monkey able to control a dial through a neuron and making it move at a different speed. Over the years, physiologist added more neurons which performed separate functions while recording several signals. Since the 1990s, EEG gained popularity and modified emerging as a solution for different groups to control devices, including paralyzed patients.

Today, EEG remains among the most common essential for different sectors, especially after the expansion of the number of controls. Mind control not only affects us but has expanded into the technology sector providing solutions to complex cases. With improvements forecast to grow EEG expensively, researchers from MIT expect to develop more mind-controlled technologies essential for manipulating more devices.

CHAPTER 2:

How to Spot if a Narcissist Is Manipulating You

Motivation speakers will always encourage each of us to develop and maintain high self-esteem. By definition, self-esteem is the evaluation of one's worth and self-acceptance. However, did you know that with excessive egocentricity mind, you may develop an ailment? It sounds awkward, but for real, unlimited, and boundless self-esteem may result in a disorder referred to as Narcissistic Personality Disorder. The illness is a disorder that is more prevalent in males than in females. As it happens to other diseases, physicians have tried to establish the leading cause of Narcissistic Personality Disorder but without success. However, it is found to be triggered by the environment, genitival, and neurobiological factors.

Additionally, some factors expose a person to the disorder. The factors include, but not limited to; firstly, exposures given to the child from the parent during the upbringing. Secondly, the gender of a person may be involuntarily factored here; a male is more vulnerable than female.

Difference between self-esteem and Narcissistic Personality disorder

Everyone in the universe will always yearn to know about the disease or a disorder he/she may be exposed to. However, when the disorder portrays similar symptoms and causes, or even definition can cause a problem in handling, preventing, and overcoming.

By definition, both high self-esteem and Narcissistic Personality Disorders are the product of ones view to self. However, one is a disorder while the other is a recommendable practice to thrive in the world full of desperations. The lack of differentiation between the narcissistic and high self-esteem will always serve as a hindrance in controlling the Narcissistic Personality Disorder. Below are things that you may check to note if you have either the Narcissist Personality Disorder or high self-esteem.

- A person with a narcissistic disorder has high regard to him or herself but do not necessarily have the self-love. Contrarily, a person with high self-esteem will first love him or herself and accept his/her current situation and in turn, have a top view of the self. Additionally, they do not feel superior to others; instead, they are contentious. In fact, if you feel offended or blissful depending on people's opinion on you, you are seemly suffering from the disorder.

- A person with high self-esteem will always yearn for a great and intimate relationship, considering they are confident. On the other hand, a person with Narcissistic Personality Disorder is found to lack interest in engagement that is intimate. In fact, they are found to seek material things and have the primary aim of proving their greatness and superiority to others. As a result, Narcissists dwell on leaving to impress rather than express, making their life more desperate and filled with anxiety.

- Persons with high self-esteem view themselves as more valuable; however, they do not contend to prove the same. On the other hand, Narcissistic Personality Disorder causes a person to crave for greatness, when not accorded one, and have the over-desires when he/she is granted one. If perhaps, after you get an accolade, you get the spirit of striving to prove more, then possibly you are suffering from the disorder.

- In summary, high self-esteem person has a positive perception of life and always content, but a person suffering narcissistic personality disorder is discontent, ungrateful, selfish, and mostly unhappy.

Causes of Narcissistic Personality Disorder

Psychologists have played a great role to establish the difference between the two. But still, to note the difference, one must be observant to the traits attached to the thought condition. The main cause of hardship in differentiating is that both deals with perception and response one may accord to the life occurrence and personal life. There are no specific causes of Narcissistic Personality Disorder; however, there are factors that trigger the condition. The condition which at times are hard to regulate is; Environment, Neurobiology, and Genetics.

Environment

This refers to the surrounding both live and non-living but impactful factors. However, the most aspect that triggers narcissistic is the weakness and gaps between the parent and the children and among the family members at large. The poor upbringing makes the child less coached to face real-life an ends up living a life full of fantasies.

Genetics

Genetics refers to the genes heredity. Particular characteristics can be passed from the parent to the generation. However, the genitival materials that get inherited from generation to another are yet to be clearly established.

Neurobiological

Narcissistically Personality Disorder affects the mental system and alters the perception and response to different things. Neurobiological refers to the connection between the behavior, thinking, and the overall function of the brain.

Factors That Make One Vulnerable To Narcissistic Personality Disorder

Firstly, the male is more exposed to Narcissistic Personality Disorder than females. Secondly, people at the teenage phase are found to be more affected than the old and very young. Thirdly, the exposure awarded to the child during the bringing up also affects the vulnerability of a person to the infection.

Symptoms of Narcissistic Disorder

Pretentious View of Self-Importance

It is worth to gain the self-importance to overcome the feeling of unworthy. However, excessive valuation of oneself can be used to denote the presence of narcissistic personality disorder. People suffering from the disorder portray the traits of arrogance, ego-centric, and ideological superiority. Additionally, the people with the disorder feel to be only understood by people of equal 'superiority' as theirs. The victims are also connected with the habit of only associating with people of high status, locations, worth, and tangibles.

Several kinds of research have also proven that the victims also expect accolades even when they have fewer qualifications or undeserving to earn any. As a result, the victims will often exaggerate their achievements and capabilities. Whenever, they conduct a talk on any issue, for example, in a relationship, they will always yearn to take the credit even when they do not really deserve. They will point out how influential their positions have been in a given relationship. They also regard themselves so unique to the extent that they refer to people in their lives as lucky to have them due to their 'great superiority.' The Narcissists are the never countered heroes and heroes, and everyone else is below them, according to their perception.

They Live In a World of Imaginations Filled With Fantasies The Fit Their Delusions Of Splendid

Due to the sense of highness and specialty, they have for themselves; Narcissists dwell in the world of fantasies since the real world cannot accommodate their wild imaginations. Narcissists spin around self-glory fantasies of bountiful excellence, brilliance, and capabilities. However, they live an unhappy life since their delusions are unattainable. For the same reason, they pile vain glory whenever a token of accolade is accorded to them.

Additionally, if they do not get the little praise from the surrounding, they crave for it to the extent of incorporating deceptions. The lies are meant to show off their capabilities, worth, and achievements. As a result, any friction and opposition against their fantasy world are countered with great thrust and even rage. So, if you happen to live around a narcissist, you should learn to work with care; otherwise, you may face the rough side of the victims' response for 'demeaning' them.

Crave for Appraisal and Delight to the Surrounding

Narcissists see themselves as more special and of great value people than others. They also regard people around themselves as lucky due to the 'value' accompanied by their presence. As a result, they require that their life be inflated with constant applause and honors to feed their ego. As a result, they struggle to live only around people who are ready to deliver their wishes. Since the narcissists are discontent, they always evaluate if the people around them are delivering the ardent wishes, and if they find that it is not happening, they regard it as a betrayal.

They Are Materialistic

Narcissists dwell on treatment accorded to them regarding their 'specialty.' They see themselves as a prince and princess who should be granted anything they need. The expectations, in turn, create anxiety which may, in turn, trigger psychological depression. Since they are enticed by entitlement, if you do not work for their every wish and whim then, you become useless, and you may be entitled to a cold shoulder and aggression. Additionally, there are attention seekers who always seek to make their presence and impact, though less is noted.

They Take Advantage of Others with Less Guilt and Shun

Due to the rating that the narcissists have on themselves, they take advantage of others for their own good. Every prince or princess feels that all the countrymen should, without compromise, subject themselves to them. Similarly, since the narcissists view themselves as superiors over others, they exploit others without guilt or shame. The act of humanity is loose, considering they only regard themselves as superior; therefore, all other people should fall under them. The main cause of the conduct is the egocentric spirit. Perhaps, a person of high self-esteem points out the erred conduct of a Narcissist; they may disregard the reprove. The reprove may be discarded in the name of the class -'*he/she cannot understand for he/she is out of our level and not classy'*. It is hard to deal with such a person. Perhaps, you are portraying similar traits; it is high time you seek for therapeutical solutions. Otherwise, you will not escape the harsh consequences of the habit.

The Narcissists Debase, Dishearten, Defame and Mishandles Others

Whenever and wherever there is a superior the opposite, inferior, must be in existence. Since the Narcissists see themselves as superior, it is absolutely sure that they may exploit, demean, intimidate, and defame others without much to worry. Additionally, they feel insecure in the presence of people who do not kowtow for them. It is evident that narcissists view themselves as superior and also contend for the same. As a matter of fact, they will enthusiastically clear and swipe away anyone who happens to be on their way to 'success.' If a high-rated person appears to them, they have the feeling of bitterness and vengeful spirit, whereas no one has offended them. Narcissists are the same character who will initiate strife even when not necessary, just to prove their worth and how great they are over their counterparts.

Persuades Of Having the Best in Life

Any person who has the disorder will be heard the longing for the best. Best car, house, and life at large. The trigger of the mind is the feeling of *I deserve the best for I am the best.'* Arguably, we all anticipate having the best in life; however, when it is excessive, it turns to be a disorder. The victim will be found to proclaim the preference he/she chooses in life. However, the favorites are of a high rating and to some extent, unattainable to the victims.

Complications Associated with Narcissistic Personality Disorder

Narcissist Personality Disorder can drag along some difficulties. Some of the effects are evident to the victims, while others are felt by the people around such a person. Such disorders include:

- Physical health problems. The victim may be experiencing physical affliction even without a notable cause.

- Difficulties in mingling with people at school and at work. Due to the feeling of superiority in the Narcissists, the conducts of the victims are not so accommodating, and as a result, they have less social impacts.

- Thoughts and acts that translates suicide. The victims will, at times, be heard to express their feeling of desperation and how neglected they feel. As a result, they think that taking their own lives will help overcome the challenges they face.

- Abuse of alcohol and drugs. The victims are always on substances that give pleasure. As a result, they end up being addicts of drugs and alcohol.

- Notable psychological depression and anxiety. Psychologists have diagnosed people with mental depression to also display similar symptoms as that of Narcissist due to the unstable state of mind.

- Physical and social difficulties. The victims are vulnerable to social rejections and physical difficulties.

How to Prevent Falling into the Trap of Narcissistic Personality Disorder

Seek Medical Aid as Soon as Possible

The symptoms of Narcissist Personality Disorder are evident. However, care must be accorded when observing to differentiate the disorder from high self-esteem principle. When the symptoms of the disorder are noted, you should seek medical attention as soon as possible to stop further negative impacts of the disorder.

Participate in Family Therapy

It also advisable that all parents do their best in attending and following the parenthood guides. It may happen that some advice may only serve as opinions; however, most of the speakers are psychologists and mental therapist. As a result, they can propose ways through which a parent may give their children a positive exposure in life. A positive exposure will, in turn, make the child live the life with reality and not just fantasies for future success. Additionally, regular and customized talks can help in educating the teens and the affected, ways to live in a healthy and more promising lifestyle.

Always Be Real and Logical

At all cost, make sure all your wishes and dreams are attainable in the real world. It has been established that at some points, we may become narcissists if we do not have control of our perception, feelings, and emotions. We all have dreams to achieve; however, make sure you set only the smart dreams to avoid the creation of the vacuum that can only be filled with a narcissistic personality disorder. Smartness, in this case, means the goal must be real and attainable.

Develop and Enhance Your Self-Esteem

The way people refer to us may not have much effect as for the way we regard ourselves. The regards we have to ourselves define our actions, perception, and responses we accord to different situations. Self-esteem refers to the status of self-contentment and willingness to improve the self without critics. The critic, in this case, means comparing yourself to others, which is abuse to you as a person. Otherwise, if you have to improve yourself, you must not be complacent. To grow, always seek to establish the loopholes in your conducts and personality and do the rectifications. Delusions are more enticing when you possess shakable self-esteem. However, with a firm foundation, you ought to dwell on reality rather than the fantasies. Established self-esteem comes with principles which make life meaningful.

Seek Contentment

The reason we wake up early and diligently work is to make ends meet. However, our needs may turn to be greed if we do not possess the contentious mind. You should always seek to be happy under all circumstances. At times we do think that if our salaries are increased, we will live well. However, the added allowances drag some other, unpredicted, responsibilities. It is wise to note that our needs can never be met wholly; therefore, contentment can work well for anyone. Satisfaction means that you strive to make ends meet, but you should be content with what you have at the end of the day. Get me right, we have to work for survival, it is a fundamental requirement, but may you not turn the need into greed.

Be Cautious of Any Habit You May Affiliate to

The people around who may have been diagnosed with Narcissistic personality disorder can show notable, but negated traits. The traits borne by the victims are uncouth and unpleasing, causing harm to the people around them. It is wise to live a life dominated by optimism and an attainable lifestyle; otherwise, we may end up being psychologically depressed.

View the Life with Real Eyes

We indeed live to make achievements; however, with a soul filled with fantasies, the vision may end up being an illusion. See the life with reality and not the wants; the truth is that narcissists are unbendable to welcome the changes. Choose a good life, a real-life, admitting the ups and downs of life.

Focus on a real dream

The anticipations for a good life are, directly, the triggers of Narcissistic Personality Disorders. Therefore, it is wise to have an established and attainable goal. Focus on the purpose and not wishes, that way, you will never have to live in a world of fantasies.

Ensure You Are in a Healthy Relationship

Be bound to the optimists and not pessimists; go-getter and not procrastinators. Narcissists cannot be able to live in a healthy relationship, the reason being that they see themselves as superiors; therefore, they cannot admit any fault. Additionally, they may fail to take responsibilities in life because they live a life beyond their reach.

Do not take all things personally

In life, once in a while, we face opposing forces; surprisingly, sometimes it is offered by the closest relates. If you decide to assume that all are meant for you, you may end up living in desperations. However, if you stop taking everything personal nothing will interrupt your inner peace and sobriety.

Set Boundaries

It is wise not to have an affordable price tag. This means that you will not be a greedy person and, in turn, you will be a compassionate person. A person with set boundaries can interact with people of a different class, perception, and dreams. On the other hand, a narcissist will only focus on high-ranked people, making it hard for him/her to mingle with fellow common men.

Device a Plan to Achieve Your Dreams

Narcissists tend to make emotions be defined by their surroundings. When they are blissful or depressed, it is as a result of what has been said, done or happened. They define themselves according to how they are perceived by others. With a set plan, the dreams can be broken down to make it achievable.

Additionally, when you look into the world with real eyes, you will be able to establish potential obstacles and device the ways to encounter them. However, for a complacent, Narcissists, person, all they live to do is a dream and fantasize more. The bigger the goal set, the higher the chances of fantasy.

CHAPTER 3:

The Art of Manipulation

The art of manipulation is a skillful tactic that most people use to get people to want to do what they want them to do. Manipulation is a convenient way for someone to get what they want without having to be persuasive. People can use manipulation either positively or negatively, depending on what they intend to achieve. In most cases, successful manipulation happens psychologically or mentally.

 Most people have, in one way or another, used manipulation at some point in their lives. This could be to either to get out of trouble or to get something they want. However, some people survive by manipulating others. Manipulation is targeted to make the victim uncomfortable if they do not do what the manipulator wants. It is most times works directly to the advantage of the manipulator and against the desires of the victim. To drive most people into manipulation, most manipulators use their passions or hobbies.

There are three main types of manipulation:

1. Negative manipulation

Negative manipulation is the most popular form of manipulation. The only person who gains is the manipulator. Intentions are always consciously malicious, mainly set to exploit someone for their gain.

2.   *Neutral manipulation*

This type of manipulation is usually unconscious. It goes in line with social expectations whereby no one intends to manipulate the other. For example, saying hello when you meet people makes it create a good relationship with people around you. When you need help, they willingly offer to help based on the link you secured. It is a constructive relationship whereby one person gives and also receives.

3.   *Positive manipulation*

In this type of manipulation, both parties are conscious of it. Both parties also benefit in one way or another. For instance, when a parent rewards a child for doing something right or when they punish the child for doing something wrong. By attaching a reward, they can make the child behave in the manner they want. By punishing the child, they instill fear of doing wrong in them, therefore preventing bad habits from recurring.

Manipulators target people with certain personalities and capabilities that allow easy manipulation. Some people are also vulnerable to allow themselves to be manipulated. People who are easily manipulated include;

- People with low self-esteem

- People who are naïve

- People who are not confident

- Dependent people

These people, in most cases, like meeting the needs of others for love and friendship. They do not easily object to the ideas of other people. They are also not able to express their negative emotions since they don't want to look bad. Manipulators take advantage of their weaknesses to use them for their gain. They mostly like using them because they are easy to control, blame, and victimize.

Predators (people who survive on manipulating others) use a wide variety of tactics to play on the minds of their prey.

These techniques include;

Lies and denying mistakes*;* Telling lies is a manipulation technique used consistently by most predators. They use lies because they have to make up stories, to make their victims fall into their traps without suspicion. They also make offenses and pretend like they do not know about it when asked. Some pretend to be extremely shocked when they are asked about it, such that the accuser/ victim believes in their innocence.

Some manipulators also pretend to be the victims so that they get compassion from the people around. Sometimes, the predators shift the blame on their victim to make them feel guilty for their mistakes. When this happens, the victims defend themselves or take the responsibility to save the situation.

Inconsistent moods and anger; Predators manage to keep their victims confused by the use of mood swings. They are able to manipulate them because the victim never knows when and how they can suddenly get angry. Because of this uncertainty, the victim tends to do everything in their ability to balance the manipulator's moods. Sometimes manipulators also use anger as a tool to stop a conversation in which they are accused. They use it to scare their victims who end up apologizing to calm their manipulators.

Administering Punishment; Punishment can be psychological or physical. Some people use silence or nagging to manipulate their victims into doing what they want. By silence treatment, they can torture the victim mentally and instill in them fear. By nagging, they make the victims give in to their demands. For example, spouses remain silent (silence treatment) on their partners to make them fear separation and negligence. Children use the nagging tactic to make their parents give them things they want.

Some predators also use physical violence to instill fear in their victims to keep them under control. This tactic is used mainly by people who fear to lose the power they have over their victims.

Sarcastic statements; Predators most often use sarcasm in front of people to lower the self-esteem of their victims. They criticize every effort by the victims to make them feel inferior. They are then able to prove their superiority and take control of their subjects.

Pretend to love and seek attention; they flatter the victim to earn their trust. They focus on this because it is always easier to manipulate people who are close to them. They seek first the attention of their target and then explain their values to penetrate their minds quickly. When they trust too much, victims lower their guard hence fall prey to the predators. Some predators also use this tactic to isolate their prey from friends and family members who might shed some light on them. By using this tactic, they are free from the blame of forcing someone to do something they did not intend to do.

Get Close and build trust; the closer the person is to you, the easier it is for you to convince them. Manipulators first make the person like them and stay close to them so that they earn their trust. Once they have their confidence, they will get easy to agree to any idea, unlike when they don't even like the manipulator. After earning their trust, predators are able to use their weaknesses to make them live as they want.

Positive perception; some time manipulators remain positive through the process of manipulation so that people they are manipulating remain unsuspecting. This perception is because people can easily forget what you say, but always remember what you make them feel. The positive input is meant to make the victim believe in their intentions, even when they are not suitable for them.

Exercising Patience and excellent listening skills; they also are patient and love the game to make persuasiveness effortless. Patience is necessary for the manipulators to be able to overcome barriers and get the right mindset in their victims. When they take time to listen, they understand their victims' objections and make them feel calm. They later use the information they have gathered to their advantage.

Giving Rewards; manipulators attach rewards to show the person that whatever it is they want them to do is also beneficial to them. For example, when bosses want employees to work extra time, they don't approach them directly with the idea. They let it out as an offer indicating a reward for anyone who will be working overtime. Through this, the employees don't feel used. Instead, they feel good about the remuneration.

By use of the above tactics, manipulators can get their victims to do what they want without suspicion or resistance.

Below are **signs of manipulation**;

Refusing to take responsibility

People who want to manipulate others never take responsibility for their actions. Instead, they twist situations to make the victims look like they caused the problem at hand. They use all possible means to make someone feel guilty for every wrong.

They refuse to honor promises

They promise to give something in return to favor or service. Once manipulators get what they wanted, they deny having made the promise. They can even pretend that they were misunderstood claiming to have said something different.

Acting the victim

They say things that make the victims feel guilty. They use this tactic to make the other person give up what they plan to do or say to please them.

Seeking attention and sympathy

They will do anything to ensure they get noticed. They go to any extremes to make sure you see their need and offer to help. When you have a problem that needs their assistance, manipulators tend to make their situations look worse. This way, you will not ask them to help you. Instead, you will sympathize with them.

Intimidation

Most manipulators rely on anger, threats, and being aggressive to make their achievements. They use these to instill fear in their targets, making it easy to control them. Fear makes the victims do what the manipulators want to them to do in a bid to make peace and avoid arguments.

Why use manipulation to get what you want? Most people manipulate others to get things to happen their way because of different reasons. The reasons, however, differ from one person to another depending on their aims.

Some of the reasons for manipulations include:

- wanting to control other people and feel dominant over them
- fear of being alone and lonely therefore get ways to make people stay with them
- lack of self-esteem, therefore, wanting to raise it by lowering that of other people
- lost hope and feeling worthless therefore seeking recognition and sympathy

Manipulators can plan to use their game for a short time or long term. When the manipulation is short term, the effects can either be short term or long term. Long-term manipulation always has long-term effects, which at times are never reversible.

People who are under manipulation cannot quickly know until the objective is achieved. When they finally realize they are being manipulated, some victims can heal the damage and move on while others remain with the hurt forever.

Let's look at some of the **effects of manipulation.**

Short term effects

When someone realizes they have been manipulated to do something, they get *shocked* and *confused* at the same time. They get surprised at the fact that a person they thought was a friend was not a true friend. The confusion comes in because they don't understand why it happened.

The person also *questions* her/ his memory, wondering whether their mind is serving them right.

Some people become *anxious* and cannot trust again easily.

Some victims also become *vigilant* because they don't want the same to happen to them again.

Shame leads to *self-blame* as they wonder why they never noticed it all along

It can also make the victim *pull themselves away* because they don't know by who and when they will be manipulated again.

Long term effects

Manipulation can lead to *isolation*. Due to the damage caused, such people tend to isolate themselves to avoid future occurrences. Such people risk leading a lonely life in the future.

People who have suffered manipulation tend to become *uncertain* of things to do in the future. This uncertainty makes them seek approval over every small matter they plan to do with fear of making mistakes.

Victims end up *turning resentful* of people who manipulated them. Other times, the resentment is transferred to people who share characteristics with their manipulators. For example, a woman who has been in a manipulative marriage end up resenting men and may never consider any relationship with men.

Depression and stress are common conditions after a period of cynical manipulation. The victims who go through extended times of manipulation slowly get stressed and depressed without their realization, when they realize, the healing process requires professional help. Some never heal entirely, and so they live with the pain all their lives.

Once manipulators succeed in making you their subject, they only stop when you realize and stop them. When some people know they are being manipulated, the effects usually have manifested, and sometimes they don't know how to handle it. The first important thing to do when someone realizes they are being manipulated is to check on their safety. When the person is sure that their safety is not threatened, they can then try to understand why the other person behaves the way they do. This is possible in instances where the manipulator does not use violence. This can be achieved through:

- Asking questions rather than avoiding situations for the sake of peace
- Being honest and direct about your opinion hence not giving space for manipulation
- Avoid doing things because you are made to feel guilty

In order to avoid manipulation in the future, you need to understand how it started and ways it happened, this way, you will be safe.

The following are tips on how to stop and avoid future manipulation.

Understand the art of manipulation. Know the tactics used by manipulators so that you watch out for signs when they show.

Watch out for people who get too close in a short time. Manipulators make you feel special so that they can know your weaknesses and use them to manipulate you.

Avoid talking too much around strangers and people who, all of a sudden, become too friendly. Manipulators ask questions and allow you time to speak more so than they can know your principal thoughts. After studying you enough, they manipulate your decisions to make you vulnerable.

Stand for yourself when you realize your fundamental rights are being abused. Don't continually compromise on the violation of your fundamental human rights to maintain a relationship.

Pay attention to how you feel. If you feel uncertain or confused, seek someone's opinions. Better still, you can back off than build a relationship that doesn't feel right to you from the beginning.

Pay attention to actions more than words. Words may lie, but actions are to be trusted. For example, when you have a concern, manipulators respond aggressively to make you enter into an argument with them. They use the case to influence your decisions by controlling your choices.

Create and maintain a distance when you realize someone has inconsistent character. Bullies tend to behave differently with you to please you and bring you close to them. Creating a distance denies them a chance to take advantage of your weaknesses.

Don't always blame yourself for all the wrongs that happen in a relationship. Assess to know if you are being treated right and whether the expectations, they have on you can be met. This way, you will not be manipulated to take somebody else's blame. If you are genuinely wrong, offer an apology and let it pass. Most bullies twist facts so that they confuse you and cause you to take the blame.

Confront manipulators any time they try their tactics on you. This will show them that you are more assertive for yourself and make them to probably back out on their tactics. In case the person in question is physically abusive, ensure your safety is guaranteed before confronting. Some of the manipulators may not take NO for an answer. The thought that they are losing control may cause them to get worse tactics. Such are the reasons we hear of domestic violence that is mentally and physically unhealthy. When things get from bad to worse, it is the best time to make critical decisions like terminating a relationship.

Negative manipulation is used to benefit one individual. Even though it doesn't leave physical scars on the victim, it can cause mental and psychological damage. For example, a husband who is not financially stable may be manipulated by the wife through intimidation. He may be required to follow instructions from the wife as she takes control of every major family decision. Even if the man does as she says to please her, he will eventually get into mental instability, which will manifest to end up in depression. In the case of extreme cases that have led to depression, it will be best to seek medical help. Complete disconnection with people who negatively manipulated someone helps with a speedy healing process.

Positive and neutral manipulation are known to leave a positive influence on both the victim and manipulator since they both benefit. For example, good managers keep their teams motivated as a part of professional development. This way, they use it as a positive manipulation tool to drive them towards their goals. This tactic helps them improve their performance leading to a smooth achievement of the company goals. The organization benefits with the productivity of the employees while they benefit through motivation tokens and appraisals. This kind of manipulation does not get anyone mentally disturbed. On the contrary, it makes life bearable for both parties.

Since manipulation is ideally a part of everybody's life, it's honorable for every person to use the positive form of manipulation. Nobody deserves to be negatively manipulated for the selfish gain of the other. It's evil for anyone to take someone through the pain of taking the blame for things they did not do. People who have been victims should also seek help, instead of becoming manipulators. It's evident that most manipulators have one time been manipulated and therefore manipulate others in a bid to feel superior. It's also advisable to stop the manipulator from getting their way with you immediately you realize they are manipulating you. This way, you will avoid the effects that negative manipulation leaves behind.

This chapter has covered the art of manipulation in details, not to arm manipulators but to enlighten the reader on how to avoid cynical manipulation. Through the understanding in this chapter, one can easily recognize when someone is manipulating them. It also guides on how to react when one realizes their predators are preying on them.

People who have not experienced negative manipulation can also benefit from this chapter. They can use the information to assess and know if they are suffering manipulation, and stay guard in case someone wants to manipulate them in the future.

CHAPTER 4:

Lies Detection: Speech Pattern Recognition and How to Stand Up Against a Manipulative Person, a Liar

Lies are all around us, and there is probably one point in time where you also lied to your family member, friend, partner, or teacher. According to research conducted, more than 91% of the total population globally lies about something. This chapter, therefore, comprises of crucial guidelines about lie detection primarily on speech pattern recognition to identify liars delivering untrue or unreliable information.

With more than eighty percent of lies going undetected, utilization of techniques such as speech pattern recognition may lower that number. Lying is a prevalent behavior to children such as eating a piece of candy and denying while still visible on the sides of their mouths. They, therefore, remain persistent on untrue information to avoid punishments leading to a continuous habit until the adult stage. While many are getting away with lies, some are easy to detect. Some become difficult to spot hence the need to adopt speech pattern recognition techniques.

Together with speech pattern recognition, this chapter also highlights different ways of how you can stand up against liars, especially on important matters such as court cases. Some lies are straightforward and require minimal experience to spot. On the other hand, others are more complicated that you may fall for and end up in trouble as well. As such, this chapter also highlights different ways of standing up against manipulative persons.

Lies Detection

Lie detection is the modern technique used to analyze an individual's verbal statements to learn if there exit any intentional deceits. Similarly, lie detection may evaluate messages and nonverbal cues as well as the questioning of psychological record to reveal falsehood and truth of responses. The most common know such activities involve the United States law enforcement utilizing lie detector machines to ascertain criminal suspects. However, the technique is rarely used in most countries as it primarily focuses on pseudoscience to generate final results.

Study and measure of deception date back the 1900s with Vittoria Benussi being the first to practice lies detection using psychological changes. He primarily focused on inspiration and expiration ratios while Burtt tested on systolic blood pressure changes. Systolic blood pressure measurements were enhanced by William Moulton Marston using a sphygmomanometer used on both student subjects and court suspects. Systolic blood pressure became widespread over time mainly used on criminals while undergoing numerous modifications.

In the twentieth century, more autonomic reactions such as pupil dilation, muscle changes, and gestures were proven to suggest cases of deception. Different devices created adopt similar responses to determine the truth among the subjects with examiners using different test techniques. Since the introduction of lie detection devices, several cases are solved each year. Therefore, judgments provided tend to be fair and useful on scientifically proven researches.

Lie Detection Techniques

Polygraph

Polygraphs detect autonomic behaviors of persons under investigation, but the outcome is often unreliable. Autonomic reactions are typically body functions not influenced by the conscious mind such as skin conductivity. Others reactions include heart rates, capillary dilation, sudden muscular reflexes, and respiratory rates. Polygraph tests, therefore, focus on these reactions where an individual wear a blood pressure gadget, pneumograph, and an electrode to determine truth.

Changes of autonomic behaviors imply that the subject shows deception to the questions. On the other hand, inconclusive results suggest that no fluctuations on the device with questions; thus, the subject tells the truth. With limited control of autonomic activities by the conscious mind, the subject is then asked questions in a controlled environment as the answer are conversant with the examiner. The widespread use of polygraph devices has gained popularity today. In the United States, different departments utilize their flexibility to ascertain the truth. Some include the Department of Defense, Custom and Border Protection and Department of Energy.

ERP and EEG

Event-Related Potentials and Electroencephalography are other techniques used to detect lies among subjects. ERP comprises of recognition assessment through the study of P3 amplitude waves generated from the brain and determine the wavelength and height. More massive waves suggest the subject sometimes recognizes with wavelengths indicate the period of the lie detection. P100 amplitude waves suggest rates of trustworthiness correlation henceforth creating a sign of lying. Similar ERP lie detection procedures have henceforth detected that immediate perpetual processes influence the detection of lies.

Like ERP, EEG focus on brain activities detected by electrodes placed on different positions of the subject's scalp. The examiner then shows images or objects to the subject, accompanied by questioning techniques to obtain recognition. Perceived trustworthiness is a crucial element to determine when the subject is lying through behavioral interpretations. According to research by Hussein, Jolij, and Binkofski, everyone has a lying and a truthful facial expression.

Eye-Tracking

Developed in the University of Utah, eye-tracking lie detection technology is a substitute to polygraph utilizing a cognitive reaction. This type of lie detection technique focuses solely on eye reactions such as pupil dilation, reading, and rereading period and errors. The subject is asked questions based on accurate and false answers and eye activities recorded on a computer. Lying remains difficult and demands a lot of effort. Henceforth, the eye-tracking method determines the hard work used, for instance, dilated pupil and taking more time before answering a question.

FMRI and fNIRS

Function Magnetic Resonance Imaging and Functional Near-Infrared Spectroscopy are two separate lie detection techniques, but both utilize brain oxygen levels. Built by Raymond Damadian in 1976, FMRI and fNIRS identify the part of the brain consuming more oxygen, called Blood Oxygen Level Dependent. Polygraphs have a limitation of detecting changes in peripheral nervous systems behaviors to determine deceptions. FMRI reveals the lies right from the brain by mounting a magnetic band on the subject's head.

With the result generated lies on the subject, finding out the truth, therefore, depends on the prefrontal, parietal lobe function. An individual is capable of telling a lie with the activation of the superior medial and cortices where FMRI and fNIRS primary focus. The technique is among the most effective and has gained popularity in other sectors. For example, the health sector, especially in the anatomical study, utilize the method to offer real-time and 3D image models of human body organs.

Drugs and Nonverbal Cues Observation

The modern world also comprises of truth drugs to extract the truth from unwilling participants. Some of the medicines included are sodium thiopental and cannabis but provide unreliable information due to the mix of fact and fantasy by the subjects. Subsequently, many people globally evaluate deception based on nonverbal behaviors such as eye contact avoidance, excessive movements, and delay responses. However, the Silent Talker Lie Detector analyzes micro-expression nonverbal activities henceforth showing either truthful or deceiving information.

Crucial Elements of Lie Detection

Begins with Neutral Questions

Before getting to the matter at hand, start by asking basic and neutral questions, which are non-threatening and straightforward. Ask about the weather, their weekend while observing their response from the baseline. When responding check on body language, eye movements, and how they construct their sentences. Asking of such questions enables you to understand some of the vital information you are to expect as an examiner.

Observe General Body Activities

When you begin asking about the essential matters, lying subjects will begin undergoing some abnormal behaviors indicating some signs of deception. Some of the common responses already highlighted include facial expression, eye movements, and pupil dilation as well as difficulty in sentence construction. Body behaviors entail liars pulling themselves together by squirming and concealing hands to hide fidgety fingers controlled by their subconscious minds.

Check Micro-Facial Expressions

There are individuals used to lying that they can control their bodily behaviors henceforth becoming challenging to observe such activities. The same applies to facial activities; hence, you may assume that they are telling the truth. Essential symptoms of deception micro-facial expressions are pupil dilation, pink skin coloration, respiratory and heart rates, flared nostrils, and rapid blinking. Tone variation and cadence in their speech also indicate the probability lies.

Speech Pattern Recognition

Speech recognition is the art of translating spoken word by the use of computers to generate text through methodologies and modern technologies under computational linguistics. As an interdisciplinary action, it incorporates different fields, such as electrical engineering and computer science. Speech recognition systems demand some skills. For instance, the recognition and translation of the text into the system with faults lead to the provision of exceptional and accurate results.

Since its incorporation in the 1970s, speech recognition encompasses patterns essential for its performance. The ultimate of the speech pattern of recognition is to create machines able to understand conversations fluently with conversational speeches as well as with complete vocabulary coverage. Models of speech recognition require powerful mathematical algorithms to solve these challenges and provide a smooth speech recognition machine.

Among the significant challenges faces in size and extent of vocabularies with most machines designed with only a 'yes' and 'no' answer. According to scientists, the future offers excellent opportunities to create devices with not only two or ten vocabularies but able to conduct full conversations with humans. Since the introduction of different patterns of words, dictionaries range from the less complicated ones to distinctive and then to the most complex.

Learning Deep Speech Recognition

Today, different devices are equipped with speech recognition capabilities and have invaded everything we use, including phones, smartwatches as well as cars. Speech recognition began decades ago but has gained popularity as developers have engaged deeper with these devices. For instance, for only $50, you can purchase the Amazon Echo Dot and speak to it effectively. The Echo Dot enables you to talk to it when making an order for pizza or to enquire for the weather report.

Over the years, deep learning has encouraged the creation of patterns making speech recognition reliable and competent. People have different ways of producing sound to develop a more realistic understanding machine during speech recognition. For a computer to listen and translate a given speech into text automatically, it utilizes different algorithms to deliver effective results.

Features of Speech Recognition Patterns

- Readily recognize and translate familiar objects w

- Recognize shapes and objects accurately from any angle

- Recognize patterns and objects quickly even when hidden separately

- Automatically identify and classify patterns

- The ability to categorize unfamiliar vocabularies or objects

Benefits of Speech Recognition Patterns

Pattern recognition paradigms have significantly assisted speech recognition in identifying and translating voice commands. The patterns are applicable in several speech recognition algorithms henceforth essential in preventing problem-related to phoneme levels. Other benefits of pattern in speech recognition entail treating massive units such as objectives and words into straightforward and real-time text patterns.

With the benefit of speech pattern recognition becoming more beneficial today, it is henceforth applied in an extensive field. Some of the areas include telephony and related domains, home automation, interactive voice response, mobile telephony, and in-car systems as well as health and military. With the utilization of different patterns, speech recognition comprises of a standard structure system. The elements involved are raw speech sampling and signal analysis, for instance, Fourier analysis, perceptional linear prediction, and linear predictive coding.

Speech Recognition Pattern Algorithms

Hidden Markov Model

The hidden Markov model is a statistical algorithm representing a Markov process in unseen states of speech recognition. The model is also presentable in the purest form of a dynamic Bayesian network with transitions connecting each step of the model. Algorithms associated with the hidden Markov model are forward, Viterbi, and forward-backward. Forward algorithms are essential for an isolated word in recognition, while forward-backward is the most vital as they aid in training a hidden Markov model. Viterbi algorithms, on the other hand, are useful in the identification of continuous speech patterns.

Dynamic Time Warping

There exist cases where recognizing isolated words require a comparison to stored words in the templates. However, the time taken to match the words with samples in the template may experience varying durations of speech due to the availability of different samples. Besides, the rate of speech may change, leading to a nonlinear alignment of the template and speech samples. Therefore, the dynamic time warping speech recognition algorithm provides solutions to nonlinear optical arrangements experienced. The algorithm measures similarities between the temporal sequences creating a constant time and speed of speech recognition.

Artificial Neural Networks

With machine learning becoming more rampant today, adoption of how the brain works also assists in creating speech pattern recognition to process the information much faster. An artificial neural networks algorithm tries to generate processors like that of the brain but much analogous. The processors, also called neurons, interconnected by links passing signals from one section to the other. The neural network, therefore, creates an artificial brain to process input data faster and produce reliable results.

How to Stand Up Against a Manipulative Person, a Liar

Manipulative persons may use some tricks to acquire what they want by using your kindness for their benefits. Liars usually have an objective of accomplishing their motives and never to be spotted as a manipulator. However, there are master liars who may become difficult for you to note and avoid. Such groups may undertake and accomplish their needs without your consent leaving you stranded and confused. It is, therefore, essential to learning different ways of noticing and avoiding such people.

Handling a Manipulator in Interactions

Remain Calm

Feeling calm is one of the essential components of dealing with a new manipulator as you have no clue on what they are up to. Many liars begin by breaking you emotionally leading you to answer to their matters irrationally. It is essential to remain calm and in control of your emotions to avoid being swept by your kindness. Take a deep breath to help in keeping you relaxed and in control.

Emphatically Say No and Stand by It

Everyone has a right to say no, especially when facing a manipulator without guilt or pity as it's your decision. Stand your ground and ensure lies do not put you in trouble or make you change your mind. Assert yourself openly and refuse to be cut off but ensure you are heard. Your response should remain firm with limited budging room making your manipulator stay back and feel you are against his or her demands.

Maintain Self-Care

Manipulators typically capitalize on your emotions to gain your trust, especially when you have low self-confidence. This strategy also involves your calmness by building a healthy self-care behavior to withstand your manipulator's exhaustion readily. Practicing mind control activities such as meditation and yoga improve your self-control henceforth creating a habit of taking care of yourself. The first impression liars approach you with is always the most influential hence remain ready to repel their charm against you.

Detecting and Facing Liars

Identify Signs of Manipulators

As liars are everywhere, it is essential to learn and understand some of their features to recognize them quickly. With their sweet tongue to create an imbalance of your agenda and benefit, noticing them earlier will prevent such situations. Manipulators frequently let you speak out first to realize your weaknesses and capitalize on them. They are also judgmental and harmful to you as well as always feeling guilty when they create a mess.

Talk About Their Behavior

When the liar who comes and interacts with you is a regular or you work with, face them, and state that you dislike their behaviors. Make it clear and strictly that they are doing wrong towards you or other people involved. Besides, you may face them as you wish as long as you drive the point against their manipulative activities. For example, if a person is influencing you to do a particular business their way, face them, and state that you are capable of doing it your way.

Highlight the Inequalities

Manipulators tend to ask for more from you with that what they deliver in return. Similarly, they may use guilt as a way of controlling you and make you feel responsible for their actions. Such people tend only to take advantage of your kindness while intentionally doing the same repeatedly. For instance, a manipulator may ask for more money or cloths after you already provided; your answer should be first to return the previous ones. As a way of standing up against them, question them adequately about the actions while eliminating yourself from the conversation.

Creation of Boundaries with Manipulators

Set Your Limits Firmly

Before engaging a liar, set clear and firm limits where your manipulator should never cross despite focusing on your kindness. Stay firm on your responses and avoid budging after you decide on a specific answer. Manipulators also understand how to get through to gain your trust, as such ensure you stand firmly on your set standards. For instance, when they request for your time to help on something for an hour, let it be an hour only without making the addition of more time.

Limit Interactions

Knowing your manipulators puts you on the forefront to limit your time and resources while interacting with them. When conducting any conversation with them, make it brief while avoiding controversial or personal topics which may land into trouble. Sometimes they may talk too much, such as gossiping, listen but minimize your responses. Such behaviors will significantly create a firm boundary between your personal or essential information from reaching such people.

Detach Yourself from Such People

Some manipulative people may cause more harm or cause severe consequences, therefore, impacting your life negatively. Others may look as food friends to you but ending making your life more miserable and uncomfortable. Despite being your friend, it is essential to say goodbye and avoid specific harmful outcomes. With friendship being a mutual relationship, you are free to make a personal decision and break up or fade out to stay away from manipulative friends.

CHAPTER 5:

Understanding Dark Psychology

Dark psychology generally studies human nature relating to one's psychological nature, allowing people to prey on others. Almost everyone in the world today has the ability to coerce other humans. Every normal human being has a predator character in them that links to their thoughts and feelings, thus practicing dark psychology. It is the science and art of manipulating and controlling a person's mindset. It can also be defined as a form of brainwashing that driven by deviant behavior. Everyone has once in their lives thought of acting maliciously towards others, something that is undeniable if people can be honest. Despite having such thoughts and feelings, some people are able to overcome and not act upon them, unlike others who will go on and hurt other people.

Having knowledge is considered as possessing some form of power; therefore, having a good understanding of human psychology is a superpower. Psychology means the ability to understand the human mind and how it operates every time. It simply explains everything and understanding it gives one the ability to influence other people. It is not very easy to obtain psychological knowledge as its information is quite hidden from the general public. To understand it fully, a person needs to dig deep into journals, books, and magazines and come up with the appropriate information.

While psychology studies human behavior centered on interactions, thoughts, and actions, dark psychology is a tactic used by people where they persuade, motivate, and coerce others to get what they want. The tactics used in dark psychology are readily found in internet ads, commercials, and even sales techniques. It is a psychiatric condition that is often passed from one generation to another. For instance, the people we trust are more likely to use the dark persuasion to get whatever they desire from us. Nobody wishes to be a victim of dark psychology, but it happens more often than we may expect. Dark psychology is not pleasant to anyone, but we cannot deny the fact that it continues to exist in the world today.

Tenets of Dark Psychology

Once people understand dark psychology clearly, the more they will be able to avoid being preyed on by their fellow humans. The following are six tenets that can help understand dark psychology much better.

It is a universal part of the human condition. This means that it is a dark side of the human consciousness and has always exerted some form of influence throughout an individual's life. Many people rarely act upon this condition; thus, are less likely to have violent feelings and thoughts. Everyone has that dark side and an unpleasant one waiting to be triggered to act.

Dark psychology closely relates to human behavior, thoughts, and perceptions that give people a chance to act maliciously upon others, thus being a study of the human condition. People always have a purpose and goal of acting in a certain way, and dark psychology assumes that there are people out there who are very close to practicing primeval evil.

Dark psychology has an assumption that everyone has the inner ability to act brutally towards other people. There are some external and internal factors that motivate the ability of a person to practice deviant and predatory behaviors. These behaviors are mostly not purposeful.

Society can be able to identify, diagnose, and eliminate the dangers of dark psychology by understanding its causes and what triggers it. One of the best things the society can do is embracing the fact that each human being has the potential to be malicious thus paving the way for those with the knowledge to come up with strategies to eliminate it by preventing it from occurring. The second thing is for people to learn and understand the basic tenets of dark psychology as it will help people to act responsibly despite the struggle of surviving.

Tactics often used in Dark Psychology

Love flooding: This is a tactic through which a person becomes overly affectionate. Overly positive compliments are made just to make a person ready to agree to a request being made.

Lying: In this tactic, lies are told, untrue stories are given, partial stories and exaggerations made. These are told in a way one can easily believe them.

Love denial: Dark psychology is practiced by withholding the affection and attention one has for the other. For the sake of getting the attention back, one is easily likely to fall into the trap of doing something they may have disagreed with previously.

Choice restriction: People practice dark psychology by giving others specific choices, thus distracting them from the particular choice they wanted to make in the first place.

Reverse psychology. In this, the victim is told to do something else that is fully contrary to what they wanted to do.

Semantic manipulation: In this case, the manipulator defines words and situations differently but makes the victim assume that words being used have common definitions. The gives meaning to the phrase that words are powerful and import.

Withdrawal. A person practicing dark psychology may tend to avoid the victim by giving them a silent treatment. This makes them give in easily, especially in love situations.

Learning to Use Dark Tactics

These dark tactics are used by people differently. There are individuals who are always aware of what they are doing trying to fulfill their purpose of getting what they want from a particular victim. Some other people are not fully aware of the dark tactics they are engaging in to get what they want.

Several people learn the dark tactics from their parents or society from their childhood days, while others learned it in their teenage and adulthood where they used the dark manipulation strategies and succeeded in getting what they wanted. People, therefore, continue to use such tactics to survive in modern days.

In other instances, people are given some training on using these tactics. Most marketing programs train people on how to use unethical persuasion tactics to make people purchase their products. The purpose is to benefit themselves and the company and not to satisfy the customer. People are convinced that such tactics are very useful, thus making use of them even in their daily lives outside the work environment.

People who commonly use Dark Psychology and Coercive Tactics

There are people in the world today who always use dark tactics to survive their way in life. The tactics have generally become part of their professional life. They include;

Narcissists: People who meet clinical diagnosis put so much worth in themselves. They always expect validation of their superiority belief from other people. They prefer using dark psychology and manipulative strategies to make people worship and adore them always.

Sociopaths: This kind of people appear intelligent and appealing; however, they are so imprudent. This is because they make use of dark psychology to build a good relationship with other people, and in the end, take advantage of them. These people usually lack emotions and do not feel any guilt after their unethical actions.

Attorneys: The main aim of attorneys is to win cases that are left in their hands. They, therefore, use dark tactics to persuade the opposing sides so that they can get the result they are aiming for.

Politicians: During political campaigns, politicians use coercive psychological strategies as a way of convincing people how good they are to work for them. The intention is only to get peoples votes and benefit themselves when they win.

Salespeople: As a salesperson, the focus is on getting more sales for better pay. In the way of motivating and persuading people to buy products, dark tactics are used. The salesperson convinces the buyer of the great benefits they will get when they purchase a certain product which may not always be true. This just happens as a way to increase their sales volume.

Leaders: In a work setting, the leaders may always use dark psychology to make sure employees comply and put more effort into their work. The intention here is just to ensure they improve their performance and benefit the company.

Public speakers: These are people who give speeches on specific topics to a set audience. Dark psychology is used in this setting, whereby the emotional condition of the audience is heightened, making them buy more products or ideas. This benefits the public speakers a great deal.

Selfish people: These are the kind of people who put their own needs ahead of those of others. They always use dark, manipulative tactics to achieve their needs first. They, at times, achieve their needs at the expense of other people's efforts. Selfish people never mind about who loses or wins in a deal as long as their needs are satisfied.

Understanding how we are Influenced by Dark Psychology

It is not a surprise to come across coercive people despite you being a nice person. These people may apply their dark, manipulative tactics to push you into a relationship before their true self is revealed. Their character may tend to vary during that moment carrying away your mind. These kinds of people only think about themselves and don't mind what happens to you in the end. Everyone has the potential of being victimized by dark psychologists. One can easily be manipulated by the use of tricks, pleasant images, and mind games played to make you comply.

The life we lead, people we interact with, and organizations we work for can condition and mold us in different ways. It is therefore important to take great care in all that we do by understanding how we are influenced by coercive forces. The following paragraphs describe how the manipulation can happen and how you can easily defend yourself.

Understanding the hidden persuaders that influence our emotions

Everyone has some hidden persuaders in their lives that make them act in a certain way. As we grow up, we tend to realize how much the environment influences our actions psychologically. We also tend to realize how much our personal needs drive our actions. Sometimes it's the people who live around us that influence us to act in a particular way, but in the end, we come to realize how much they played with our psychology and making us do things we may never have thought of doing.

The manipulator may come up with the same idea but in a different way, and we are still likely to fall for the trap. This is because they have the skills to coerce people to do as they wish emotionally. For instance, a cult manipulator may order people to drink poison and die after first giving the poison to their children. This is an extreme trap, but due to the power, this man has many people who are not strong enough may definitely fall for the trap. People who were strong enough and had the desire to see their relatives and themselves live may not easily fall for the trap. This is because they believe they are not crazy enough to be influenced by a fellow human being to kill their own children.

To defend yourself from such dark psychological tactics, it is important to learn and understand how the mechanism works. The benefit of this is that you will be strong enough to overcome coercive psychological manipulations as well as the psychological conditions that you may experience every day. You will be able to control these forces and achieve freedom over your own life. This is because a manipulator will always study how vulnerable you are to being coerced to engage in a certain act.

Being aware of the individuals that give you what you want

People who you see as your friends will always be your friends, those you see as your parents will always be your parents, and those you see as mentors will always be your mentors. It is important always to understand how you are relating to people in your daily life to avoid being a victim of dark psychology. Whenever the deal is too good, always think twice. People may come to you with too many promises, and fulfillments of things you had lacked previously this may make them look pleasant getting you much closer to them. However, you should be very careful not to fall into their hidden agendas. Always think beyond what they are offering to understand their motive and true nature. Do not easily trust anyone because they offer you what you have been desiring.

Understanding your Primal Human Needs

Our personal needs can either be fulfilling or destructive to ourselves. It is important to ensure that all your psychological and physical needs are met to avoid falling into the traps of human predators. Having a good understanding of your personal needs makes it easier for you to beware of the happenings of an event and ways in which you can control and overcome the situation to avoid being manipulated into doing something you may not like. It will help you give an appropriate response to anyone who tries to convince of fulfilling your emotional needs with the intention of gaining some power over you.

Understanding your needs is advantageous in that you will not easily be attracted to coercive tactics that promise to provide things that you are lacking. It is important to ensure that you are giving and receiving adequate attention, the environment you are living in is secure enough for you to develop, you have a positive emotional connection with other people, you are interacting with the right friends, having adequate love and intimacy and that you have a sense of status and belonging in all social group you engage in. It is easier for you to satisfy these needs without being coerced to act in a particular way to satisfy them.

Coming up with rational arguments for anything you are told

Our thirst for some needs can make us susceptible to coercive tactics of people who promise to offer to provide the need. This is because everyone strives to get quality attention, and it is important to use the conscious mind to come up with questions on why you should do as you are asked to do. It is important that you have an open mind to understand how your emotions can possibly be used against you. For instance, when you are thirsty and, in a desert, it is easier for you to be coerced to consume any form of liquid in a bid to save you. It is therefore important to beware of how you can deal with the situation without being forced to do something unthinkable.

Making a commitment and being consistent with it but Remaining Flexible with the Ideas you make

It is often evident that whatever we say, we are likely to think it and stick by it. Once you verbally commit or write down an idea, there are high chances that you will honor it. In cases we do it publicly, we would always want other people to see our consistency thus committing to the idea. However, it is important to remain flexible and change your mind whenever possible. This way, you will be able to realize when you are being fooled and avoid negative outcomes.

Avoid following the Crowd

In many cases, you may be a victim of social proof where you think that a thousand people cannot be wrong. To defend yourself from dark psychology, it is wise not always to follow what everyone else is doing. This is because you can blindly fall into some dark tactics. It is important that you watch what has happened to people who acted in a certain way and derived some lessons from that. Always try to understand how these dark psychological tactics are applied to persuade people to act in a certain way. We should not always act because other people are acting.

Avoid being Blindly Obedient to the Authority

Obeying authority is one of the most important things to help one succeed in everyday life. However, do not be blinded by the fact they are the bosses, and you have to do as they say. It is important that you give consideration of what the authority is asking you to do before doing it. Understanding the dark psychology mechanisms authorities use is important to enable you to make a decision about whether you will do it or not. Always give a second thought to all commands they give and look on both the positive and negative sides of following the commands. This way, you cannot be easily manipulated to do something unthinkable.

Do not Judge a Book by Its Cover

People who apply dark psychology when manipulating people may always seem so nice. Attractive people are easily likable, making it much easier for them to persuade you. This is because they are considered intelligent and smart. However, it is not guaranteed that good-looking people will always have good intentions. Take great precaution before thinking of buying an idea or product from a person because they are attractive. It is good that you question their nature before assuming they have positive intentions.

Keeping it simple

It is important you defend yourself from coercion by human beings and organizations by simply understanding the basic tools used in manipulating people. These are; the threat of losing something valuable or an important person and being promised to gain something of great value. These two powerful tools can easily change your behavior and belief, thus blindly following a person's ideology. Secondly, always stay calm when faced with a challenging situation. When your mind is calm and settled, you can easily think about something you are told and easily come up with a solution whether to follow it or not. You will be able to calculate the risks of ideology and how you can evade the. By doing so, you can defend yourself from becoming a victim of dark psychology. It is also important not to mock other people who may have fallen into traps unknowingly but to guide them on what to do to avoid such experiences again.

CHAPTER 6:

How Psychology Can Help You to Detect

a Deceptive Fellow

The human mind is the most unique component of the whole system of the body. The brain controls even the function of the most insignificance part of the body. However, to some extent, we cannot decide how to react, non-verbal communication when performing some action. As a matter of fact, it is easy to know a timid or a deceiving person from the look of his non-verbal expression than to listen.

In the twenty-first century, some deception may not succeed, no matter how good they may be cooked. Psychology, the study of the human mind and its function, has advanced day in day out. From the study, psychology has revealed that there are particular physical reactions done by the body when a particular action is performed. However, the actions are done involuntarily, making them useful to detect the authenticity of the information being passed by a particular person.

Is It Worth To Know How Your Brains Operate?

It can be considered as a high rate of arrogance if we just live to assume why and how some things happen to us. It is well established that whatever and however, your body does, the command comes from the mind. Understanding our mind helps us to know how to combine the two, conscious and unconscious mind to make life meaningful. Regarding our topic, you too have to understand the essential operation of the mind to know how to interpret different responses showed by a person.

How the Human Brain Operate

The human brain is the most complex organ in the human body. Surprisingly, we all own it, even with less understanding of it. The main difference between the brain and mind is that, in computer terms, the brain can be regarded as the hardware while the mind, software. However, they are inseparable. The best way to precisely describe how the human mind works are by comparing it with a computer. However, I think the analogy of computer was deduced from how the human mind operates. Basically, human consciousness can be categorized into two major groupings, namely, Unconscious and the Conscious mind.

Limbic Brain System

Limbic brain system can be defined as, in layman's language, the unconscious part of the mind. This part of the mind is believed to have 90% of the total functionality of the human mind.

We all do things that we often do mindlessly, yet they are vital, and without them, we cannot exist. For example, when did you last remember not to forget to breathe! The absolute answer is - I do not know. Therefore, we have some functions of the brain that are basic but out of our control. Some of the functions include:

<u>Breathing</u>

For any living creature, inhalation and exhalation are vital things for survival. The body takes in oxygen only to produce out the Carbon dioxide. Surprisingly, we do not have to take note of each of the step taken in the process. Therefore the whole process happens involuntarily. Deep and shallow breathing can be used to indicate the authenticity of the information provided. Whenever a person is in a tensioned environment, the breath is so first to an extent you can quickly note

<u>Digestion</u>

Do you live to eat or eat to live? That is a question asked by most of the nutritionist. The primary purpose of the question is to instill the notion of, and it is not a matter of eating to satisfy our feelings but our body. However, the moment we ingest food and boluses pass through the trachea through the peristalsis process, the only thing we note is when our bellies have an upset. We do not have to keep turning and checking on the food to be digested, how amazing the creation is! The work is done involuntarily, without our actual intervention. The nutritionists will always advise you to drink water, after and before eating to help in the digestion process. However, we have to be told how the fluid will aid in digestion, for even after drinking, we do not know the actual relationship between the two: Digestion and the water. Therefore, even if we are advised to do some routines to help our body function well, we have less to do after we swallow. In fact, the body can reject any material consumed through vomiting.

<u>Sleeping</u>

Have you ever wondered what happens when immediately after and before when you get to sleep? After the toiling and working for a long time, our body needs to rest. That is the reason you hear someone saying, 'I feel dizzy.' The feeling is automated that, whenever the body gets fatigued, there is a need to rest. To prove that sleeping is out of control, the sleep is sometimes referred to as half-death. I think, just think that the evil men use this analogy to spray some active chemicals that induce sleep because you can do nothing while asleep.

Heart rate

Biology and other scientific studies have always insisted to us that the heartbeat for a healthy heart is 72 beats per minute. However, the beat is altered by our emotions, when in great wrath, fear, and uncertainties. The heart rate does not change with ranks, race, or social classes, because nobody can control them.

Temperature control

The body has its own mechanism to control the temperature. The control of temperature is done by the hypothalamus. Hypothalamus induces occurrences that help the body to remain in its average internal temperature even if that of the environment changes. Such occurrences include; sweating, shivering, erection of body hair, among others. All of this cannot be controlled by our mere interventions. Though we have to cover our bodies at night and wear light clothes during hot days; that is less compared to what happens in the body. Psychologically, a person who is under tension will have his or her body temperature elevated. The increased temperature can even lead to sweating uncontrollably, and this can be used to detect a lying person

The reactions and emotions you ever grant to a situation is decided by the brain

What if I step on your toe intentionally! Will you take minutes thinking about what to do? The fact is that emotions will take over even before you think about it. That is the work of the unconscious mind.

Imaginations and illusions all originate from the mind

We all have wishes and hopes for a good future. At times we can see ourselves driving the most expensive car, living in a luxurious house and life at large. However, this all happens in our mind, we imagine and illuminate things we are thinking about. We, literally, do not need to tune the kind of imaginations we have we only have to take it that way.

The Mind Establishes And Maintains The Habit That The Whole Body Adheres To

We all have perception and responses, tuned differently. To some extent, the habit we assimilate to is dictated by our environment, our efforts, and what we feed our mind with. However, after the mind is tuned by the mentioned factors, we have less to control, in terms of habits.

The mind Controls the reflex actions

How many minutes do you take to respond after you get hold of a hot object? Absolutely nanoseconds, this is because the body responds without your consent when a need calls. The response is referred to as reflex action.

The Mind Serves To Store And Retrieve The Information In The Long Term Memory

We forget what we do not want to and remember what we want to forget, some will say. However, psychologists have proven that if an issue, occasion, or just anything is in mind for more than two minutes, it is stored in the long-term memory. When we face a great loss or achievement, we find ourselves thinking about it all day long. As a result, the information gets stored in long-term memory.

The Conscious Mind

Conscious literally means that the action can be controlled. All human beings are subjected to decide to do good or evil. As a result, the conscience of a person judges and discerns if whatever has been done was right or wrong. It is believed that the conscious mind caters for only 10% of the complete functionality of the mind. The conscious mind is that which we use on a daily basis to determine how, when, and what to do at a particular time. The main functions of the conscious brain are:

Gathering information: We get informed day by day; at times, we need to know about the unanswered questions. The mind is involved in identifying the corresponding facts.

Evaluating and analyzing the data collected: After the collection of data, the conscious mind interprets the meaning attached to each bit. However, the interpretation is influenced by our stored knowledge.

Establishing the comparison between the data collected: The level of understanding and the abilities of the human mind are referred to as IQ, intelligence quotient. The conscious mind is mandated with retrieving the already stored information to help understand and establish a relationship with the found data. I think this the same reason we regard the old people as wise because they have seen and experienced much.

Resolving matters and granting the orders: Normally, we judge people according to their level of understanding. The brain of a young child is less developed, and the resolving of critical matters is tough for them, that is the reason why they need the guardians. The Conscious mind is the one responsible for finding a solution to given problems and seeking a reaction for the same.

Supervising the short-term memory: Any information that is being used by the mind is stored in the short memory. As in the case of a computer here, we have the Random-Access Memory. The conscious mind is the one responsible for the storage and retrieval of the required information from the short-term memory.

The Science Behind Any Lie

We interact with people who have different principles, ethics, and conducts. To maintain the relationship we have, some people will formulate some mockery phenomenon to kill our suspicion. Lies can be told for different purposes: the desire to prove innocence, to maintain social interaction, to avoid conflict, and to gain the interpersonal power. A lie is a statement that has been made intentionally, but it is not wholly accurate.

Types of Lies

The lie is categorically placed as a type of behavior and thus referred to as aversive interpersonal behavior. However, depending on the situation, the liar, and the story behind, the lies can be categorized into three: white, real, and grey lies.

<u>White lies</u>

A white lie is the most common in most of the people. The reason being it is meant to justify and injure any person. As a result, many people will frequently lie. Most people refer to it as tactful lies since it can be used as a scapegoat with little moral input. The lie can be used to protect the image of a person and maintain a stable relationship.

<u>Real lies</u>

Have you ever decided to purchase a commodity on a shelf but the issued commodity is not as good the one you saw? That is an example of a real lie. A real lie uses a real occasion to deceive the victim about the current situation. Therefore, for real lie, the statement made by the liar can be very true but does not fit the context you may be negotiating on.

<u>Grey lies</u>

As the name suggests, it a most treacherous ay of deception in that it combines both the white and real lie. It could be hard to identify one but, because all are lies psychology can be used to detect them.

Actions That the Body Does Involuntarily and Can Be Used to Detect Lies

<u>Handshake</u>

Traditionally, the greetings were conducted via shaking of hands. The fact makes it more effective due to less suspicion from the liar. It has been established that the way people shake or respond to a handshake can portray their feelings.

A courageous and innocent person will respond well to a firm handshake, which is opposite to a guilty person. There are some characteristics that can be deduced from the handshake, which can be useful to the detection. These include; temperature, grip, strength, vigor, and the eye contact.

The persons who are described to have a firm and grip handshake are considered more open and transparent.

The grip applies to the duration a participant is comfortable with. This is because a lengthy handshake will expose the reality of the person. It is also advisable to maintain eye contact with the person to make the detection much more comfortable and promising.

<u>Body orientation</u>

The human mind controls all the functions in the body; therefore, with guilt, much is exposed to portray the status of the mind.

Variation of the voice: The confidence of a person can be deduced from the voice. For any deceiving person, there is a portion of his/her conscience that shows the guilt; as a result, inconsistence of voice can be detected easily.

The mannerism and voice of a person telling a lie to deviate from the normal. To detect the flow, you may pose specific and easy questions to the suspect. The questions may include, but not limited to, the name, residence, likes and dislikes, and their interests. The interview will help you to identify if the person is truthful. It will be sure that the person is lying when the voice changes from the initial and the mannerism in which the person talks changes to show discomfort.

A Lying Person We Expose His/her Discomfort: Most people are aware that their presentation can induce suspicion. As a result, a liar will always try to be comfortable so as not raise suspicion from the subject. Due to the tension and nervous status of the person, they will try to minimize movements, stay calm, and with keenness, you can identify the facts. The notion behind this clue is that, in a normal situation, a person will be relaxed and this can be shown by their body movement like gestures. For a lying person, mostly, they pull both limbs towards the body.

A mismatch between the words and expressions: Whatever is said via mouth has first to be interpreted by the mind. As a result, all other body parts work in harmony to convey the message. Therefore, it is easy to detect a liar in that the message and expressions, particularly facial, do not match. If the message is supposed to induce joy, the person will display a face that is half smiling and half frowning.

Change In The Way Of Communication: The person may change the language of communication to make the latter distance him/her from the truth. For example, if the statement was 'I saw her purse, but I was not sure it was hers' is changed to 'I just a saw purse and...' The main cause and reason for changing question are to avoid questions such as 'How did you know it was hers?' As an interrogator, you should base on the first statement as it is always the truth, before the alteration by the guilt.

A Liar Is Always Not Comfortable To Face You Directly: There indeed exist shy and timid people; however, genuine timidity can be easily differentiated from guilt shyness. According to investigation officers, a liar will always face the sides away from the interviewer while the eyes work as if searching something. To avoid inappropriate judging, it is established that anyone who is trying to recall will face up and if to the sides the eyes are at a fixed position, which is not the case to a guilty person.

Movement of Hands: Due to the guilt, the interviewee can be seen covering the eyes or mouth with the hand after a certain leading question has been asked. The covering is accompanied by an expression of wonder. Alternatively, the suspect might close the eyes while talking, particularly when responding to a sensitive question.

Inappropriate Gestures: Gestures are the reflection of what the interpretation of a phenomenon was perceived from the mind. Since the guilt affects the state of expression, the suspect will portray actions that are triggered by anxiety. Such activities include;

licking the lips, looking at the nails or random shaking of the head. The actions result from the reactions that try to calm the soul from anxiety.

Notable pauses during the talk: It is advisable to let the interviewee do the most of the talks. This gives him/her a length to 'finish' the cooked lies. As a result, a liar will take several pauses trying to connect the words in a way they will cause less suspicion. To counter, you may pose a few questions using the words the suspect used to cover the gaps left during the interview.

Talk too much but giving unnecessary information: Whenever a question is posed, it is observed that the suspect will give much explanation. The explanations have some points of justifications attached to them. The suspect may indicate how reformed or innocent he/she has been. The exaggerated responses are meant to detach the suspect from the guilt he/she is having. Additionally, a liar will try to prove why the statements made are not cooked.

Way of walking

The stagey walking of a person may indicate a lack of confidence. When a deceiving person is approaching you, the walking style is not consistent; however, if it is, the constraints can be observed. The person walks with head jerked back to face up or facing downward or tilted to the side. The reason is that the person does not have the confidence to meet you directly.

Additionally, the person walks with raised shoulders to assure his heart that the guilt is absent. However, all of these acquired posters fade when a question is posed, or the person is getting ready to answer a question.

In summary, to avoid misjudging the innocent, it is wise that you apply the observation so keenly. We have people who can display characteristic of guilty persons while they are still innocent. Therefore, before making any conclusion, make sure you consider all the factors that can invalidate your observation.

CHAPTER 7:

Emotions

Emotions always play a significant role in controlling human behavior. The way we act significantly depend on the kind of emotions we have and the strength of our emotions can either make us avoid events we find pleasure in or do things that you do not usually do.

According to psychology, an emotion is a multifaceted kind of feeling that leads to both psychological and physical changes that determines the thoughts and behaviors of an individual. Emotions manifest opinions that cannot be expressed verbally such as disagreement, agreement, embarrassment, love, interest, or hate.

Emotions can also be described as affirmative or destructive experiences linked to some physiological activities. Emotions bring about various cognitive, behavioral, and physiological changes in an individual. They are the responses a human being gives essential events, both internal and external. The emotions are mainly derived from the circumstances and moods in which people relate with others.

In psychology, emotions contain coordinated responses including, behavioral, verbal, and physiological mechanisms. They can be dispositions, occurrences, short-lived, or long-lived. All emotions generally exist in a variety of intensity. Other fields define emotions as the kind of feelings we direct to other people or something we come across. They describe how we react to everything we face as we go about our daily tasks.

Practically, emotions are defined as an outcome of a process that is both conscious and cognitive, and that occurs as a way of responding to a body system when it reacts to a trigger.

Components of an Emotion

There are five significant elements of emotions that researchers have found to exist. All the elements must be coordinated for a feeling to be expressed. They include the following.

Cognitive appraisal. This element plays a significant role in evaluating an event or object.

Bodily symptoms. These are the physiological elements that describe the kind of emotional experience a person gets.

Action tendencies. These act as a motivation that gives direction on how one responds to an occurrence or object.

Expression. Some verbal or physical expression always accompanies the emotion. These expressions help in communicating how a person feels about another person or object.

Feelings. These are the experiences one gets after an emotion occurs. They are subjective.

There are three essential parts of emotion.

The subjective component. This describes how an individual experiences emotion.

The physiological component. This portrays the reaction of our bodies to an emotion.

An expressive component. This shows the behavior we portray when reacting to emotion.

Purpose and Value of Emotions

Emotions tend to play significant roles in a person's life. This is because they help a person come up with some strategies on how to respond to both internal and surrounding obstacles. In ancient times', emotions helped in coming up with solutions to challenges that ancestors occasionally faced.

However, in the modern days', emotions also have some negative values to human beings. This is because some emotions bring about anxiety causing mental illness to an individual.

Classification of Emotions

Emotional episodes and emotional dispositions are much different in making a distinction from one emotion to another. Emotional disposition is much similar to the character traits of an individual. They are the emotions a person shows anytime they are faced with a particular situation or object. They mainly depend on the physiology and genetics of a person, thus being linked to personality. Emotional dispositions help us to understand the decisions people make in different occurrences. On the other hand, emotional episodes are occurrences. These are, for instance, panic, a sudden feeling of fear.

Basic Emotions

Paul Ekman outlined the six primary emotions a human being experiences. These are anger, disgust, happiness, fear, surprise, and sadness. According to Ekman, all these emotions are universal, and almost every culture embraces and accept them. Later in his researches, he added other emotions expanding the list. These emotions included awe, embarrassment, pain, desire, amusement, sympathy, sadness, and relief.

Robert Plutchik came up with a wheel of emotions in a bid to advance the work of Paul Ekman. He came up with a model that helped to describe both positive and negative emotions basis. He grouped the emotions as follows; trust versus disgust, anger versus fear, joy versus sadness, and surprise versus anticipation.

Coordination of basic emotions leads to complex emotions. This way, they bring about a whole experience one gets leading to either positive or negative outcomes.

Roles that Emotion Serve

Emotions motivate an individual to take action. There are many instances in which emotions help us to act on something to get some positive outcomes. For example, when you are faced with stiff competition in a table tennis game, you are likely to experience some form of anxiety on how well you will perform and receive a scholarship that had been promised to the winner of the game. Such emotional responses will make your practice more on the game.

That emotion motivates you in taking action by doing the positive thing so that you can win and receive the scholarship award. In many cases, people will always act to get some positive outcomes and eliminate the potential of negative emotions.

Emotions help people to survive, thrive, and avoid danger. There is a significant adaptive role that emotions always play in every living thing. Human beings, for instance, will avoid getting into negative emotions that may reduce their chances of survival and thriving in every activity. For example, when feels fear, they are likely to escape from the threat.

Emotions always play a significant role in helping us make decisions. Our feelings significantly influence the decisions we make in everyday life. Our choices are not always guided by our rationality and logic but considerably by the emotions we experience. While making a decision, the ability we have in understanding and managing an event plays a vital role. Negative emotions may influence you to make poor decisions while on the other hand, positive emotions may lead to ethical decision making.

The emotions we experience help other people understand us much better. Anytime we interact with people; our feelings will always help them understand how we feel towards something or people. During this interaction time, your body language and verbal expressions always describe the emotions we are getting. This way, other people will be able to understand us better and know how to act or what to say or avoid doing when we are with them.

Emotions also play a crucial role by allowing us to understand other people. Emotions not only help other people perceive us but help us know them too. The emotions that people around us express gives us more knowledge about who they are. This is because when a person shows a particular passion, we can interpret it and understand why they have reacted in a certain way, thus knowing how to respond to them. This way, deeper and healthier relationship is built leading to societal cohesion.

Theories of Emotions

Psychological researchers have immensely worked on developing several assumptions that explain the rising of human emotions and representing them to the brain. The significant theories on emotions are divided into three divisions. These are:

- Physiological methods. These theories are based on the fact that emotions are responsible for the responses that occur in our bodies.

- Neurological theories. The theories explain that there are activities that take place in our brains that influence our emotional reactions.
- Cognitive theories. They are based on the argument that when emotions are being formed, thoughts and mental activities play significant roles.

The following are some of the theories that describe emotions:

Evolutionary Theory of Emotions

Charles Darwin did great research on how emotions evolve. He tried to express the idea that sentiments can be adopted and always play a significant role in helping both humans and animals reproduce and continue surviving. The adoptive part that emotions always act as motivations for us to respond to a trigger in the surrounding. This way, people can thrive and continue surviving. People can escape danger by understanding the emotions of others and fleeing from the threat itself.

The James-Lange Theory of Emotion

This happens to be one of the popular physiological theories of emotions. William James was the man behind the creation of this theory. Two physiologists,

William James, and Carl Lange proposed the theory. Basing from their independent ideologies, James-Lange theory explains that how we physiologically react to events determines the emotions an individual experiences. An external trigger causes a physiological reaction through which emotional response is based. An example of defining to understand this theory better is when a person is trimming a fence and sees a vast chameleon. The person may start trembling, and the heart beats faster. The person will conclude that they are frightened. Basing on the James-Lange Theory, being frightened causes the trembling and the heart beating faster.

The Cannon-Bard Theory of Emotion

This theory contradicts the James-Lange theory of emotion. According to Cannon, the physiological reactions that people experience may have some connections with emotions but are not directly caused by their feelings. An example is when the heart beats faster than usual; it is not necessarily because a person is frightened or afraid but may be due to some physical activity a person had been engaging in.

The Cannon-Bard Theory, therefore, proposes that we instantaneously experience emotions and physiological reactions. For instance, being frightened and trembling to occur at the same time. The theory tries to explain that the occurrence of a feeling and physical reaction happens at the same time and that none depends on the other.

The Schachter-Singer Theory

This is a famous example of the cognitive theories of emotion. According to the theory, for an individual to consider an occurrence as an emotion, physiological stimulation initially occurs, and the individuals try to understand why it has happened. The theory is mainly based on the presence of the situation and the cognitive definition used to name the emotion. The method also bases its arguments on the idea that different circumstances can lead to different types of emotions. An example is sweating during a job interview; the feeling may be described as anxiety. The same may be experienced when going on a trip abroad; the emotion can be described as joy.

Cognitive Appraisal Theory

According to this theory, a person initially thinks before they experience emotion. The expert in coming up with this theory was Richard Lazarus. The theory describes the pattern of events before one experience a feeling. The first thing to occur is the trigger, and thought follows. Whatever a person thinks leads to the physiological response and feelings that arise at the same time. An example is when trimming the fence and come across a chameleon; the first thought is that you are in danger, which leads to some fear as the emotional reaction leading to physical responses. In this case, you may either decide to fight the chameleon or to flee from the place.

Facial-Feedback Theory of Emotion

According to this theory, the facial expressions people portray are directly linked to the emotions they are experiencing. A change in the face muscles always expresses how a person feels about a situation. For instance, when attending a social gathering, and the person puts on a smiley face, the whole event is likely to be enjoyable. On the other hand, a frowned face will describe the event as annoying and not pleasant. Emotions always play a significant role in explaining how positively or negatively human beings view the world.

Signs of Positive/Negative Emotions

Positive Emotions;

Positive emotions can be described as any feelings whereby negativity is not experienced. Some of the most common positive emotions include; interest, pride, inspiration, gratitude, joy, serenity, love, and awe. The following paragraphs briefly describe the positive emotions.

Serenity: It is a state of satisfaction in what you have. In this case, a person is much contented with the little, or much they have and never feels like they should always benefit from fate. The best thing about serenity as an emotion is that a person remains calm.

Interest: interest plays a significant role in helping people achieve the goals they have set to meet their particular needs. Attention gives one a chance to explore the happenings of the world, thus being able to discover a lot of useful things.

Joy: It is one of the most positive emotions people experience. Joy describes a state of bliss, happiness, and general comfort. Being joyful in different situations helps people to find overall satisfaction in life.

Amusement: In this case, people tend to avoid taking events and situations too seriously. Entertainment, as a positive emotion, is experienced when something sounds funny, especially humor. To experience this emotion, one should always try to find happiness in everything they make even the mistakes they make. This way, one can live happily throughout their lives.

Awe: This is a positive emotion that people portray when they come across something appealing. For instance, when one is shown, some custom made pillowcases, they marvel at the designer and appreciate their work. Generally, when people think of all the good things in life, they may show a positive emotion of awe.

Elevation: `this is a kind of positive emotion that people show anytime they see other people taking part in acts of kindness.

Positive body language. These are the non-verbal signs that communicate positive energy when listening to another person. They include the body movements and gestures made showing interest in whatever is being said. These signs help the speaker always to use words that continue pleasing the audience.

Keeping eye contact: the signals a person sends using their eyes always have a significant impact. Maintaining eye contact is shows positive emotion in that it expresses the confidence and sincerity of an individual. It also helps to prove one is really listening and responding positively to what a person is saying.

They are showing a sense of gratitude. A person with positive emotions is always thankful for whatever they have in life. Recognition acts as a sign of positive emotion in that a person finds it easy to appreciate fellow human beings and things around their life. They can relate well with other people as a sign of showing them they are playing significant roles in their lives.

Ability to cope with emotions: It is never a guarantee that one will always experience good things in life. A person with positive emotions can embrace any challenges in life and not allow emotions to stand on their way. They ensure they do not cause any chaos in the interactions they make.

Capability to love. Love is one of the most potent positive emotions a person can show. People with positive emotions can show love selflessly to everyone in their lives.

Ways to Develop Positive Emotions

Having positive emotions not only feel good but helps you lead a happy and comfortable life. The following are three ways through which people can be able to develop positive emotions in their lives.

Identifying and keeping track of positive emotions. A person should be able to specify whatever makes them happy in their everyday life.

Focusing on a particular positive emotion and acting to advance it. Once a person identifies the main factor that causes happiness, they should practice on it more to continue developing it.

Using a positivity treasure chest to boost oneself.

Negative Emotions

These are the feelings that make one feel sad and miserable in life. Negative emotions always impact the life of a person negatively by making them lose confidence in themselves. People with negative emotions tend to dislike themselves and never believe in their abilities to handle various situations. The following are some of the signs of negative emotions.

Negative body language. The movement of a body can express the negative emotions a person may be experiencing from a situation. The body movements of a person can express a lot about how they feel about a situation more than even words can say.

Avoidance of eye contact. When ones were making eye contact during communication, it may show a feeling of discomfort and anxiety. Being unable to make eye contact may also reveal the presence of fear, for instance, when someone is lying.

Crossed arms: in cases where people communicate while their arms are crossed may be a sign that they are not comfortable with the person they are talking to. They may be feeling some form of barrier while talking to the other person. It portrays a negative emotion of lack of friendliness and openness.

They are frequently looking at a watch, phone, or clock. When people keep on checking their watches or phones during a conversation, it is evident they are not interested in the topic and would like it to end quickly. This kind of people usually suffers anxiety and impatience as they always think of what they are supposed to do next and not what is currently happening.

Frowning. This is one of the most common signs of negative emotions. Frowning describes feelings of sadness, anger, discontent, or even sympathy. Frowning is seen when a person forms a facial expression when the face appears wrinkled or stiff as the speaker continues with their speech. A person may frown whenever they feel as if a specific address is directed to them, thus experiencing emotions of anger and discontent in the address.

Dealing with Negative Emotions

We all must understand that negative emotions are part of our lives, and this way, we shall be able to overcome them.

Change what you can. It is essential that as an individual, you change on the things that make you experience negative emotions quite often. This can be done by always communicating whenever something is not favoring you. Communication is the key to help people understand you and what fits your specifications. Changing a pattern of negative thoughts through self-cognitive restructuring can also help overcome expressing negative emotions.

CHAPTER 8:

Using NLP to Protect Yourself

NLP stands for neuro-linguistic programming, which is a technique formulated to help a person in personal development through communication. The founder, John Grinder, established that there is a connection between neurons, language, and the pattern of behavior (programming). To make the establishments, Grinder observed keenly on different occurrences to make some conclusions. That fact makes his findings logical and practical since it was not made in the laboratory; it was an actual experiment. The main intention of the invention was to help model skill and stability with self. The achievement can impact the development in a corporate relationship and business success.

How to Protect Yourself Using Neuro-Linguistic Programming (NLP)

Dissociation

We, at times, get entangled in situations that make us constrained. In a caged condition, our potentials cannot be fully extracted. This is because the position controls our perception and turns the behavior. According to NLP techniques, you should have a free space to exercise your capabilities and at the same time feel comfortable. The process is simple:

Firstly, identify the situation that causes the discomfort and the one that you are willing to discard. Secondly, take the position of an observer and look back to your life and the circumstances you have coped with.

Thirdly, you will start to notice a change - a change in your feelings.

Fourthly, you have made the achievement because the dissociation removes the negative emotions.

The dissociation makes you free from anxiety and guarantees, gaining a positive perception. In layman's language, separation is detachment from an established situation, location, or position, which is possibly the source of anxiety and panic. The technique literally means that you remove your 'current you' and became a 'new you' by observing your situation as a third party, away from the actual position. The reason you should assume the third party position is that, if you search for a solution while still in the 'current you' there are many possibilities of making excuses. Excuses will, in turn, affect the decision to resolve your problem, and perhaps a solution is sought, there are chances of biases.

An intentional dissociation from the entangling situation will help you create a solution from a neutral ground. Dissociation is the best remedy whenever you feel anxious about the situation.

<u>Content reframing</u>

Whenever you have a feeling of negativity and helplessness, seek to apply this technique, content reframing. It refreshes your soul and mind by eliminating the negativities.

For example, you may encounter a loss; your car got stolen. You will indeed have to think about, but did you know the result is depression and anxiety. In fact, you should deduce a positive aspect of fate. No one will promise that the process is easy, but it is worth it. Perhaps, after the loss, you may sit down and deduce the advantages of walking or taking public transport. The benefits of walking are that it is a good of regulating body weight. Walking reduces the unsaturated fat in your body; unsaturated fat can lead to obesity and heart attacks. On the other hand, using public transport saves on fuel and environmental degradation.

Focusing on fear and panic will only create more problems. In contrast, focusing on the solution and reframing the content makes you responsible and able to overcome the situation.

Content reframing is as simple as you take and comprehend it.

Firstly, identify the situation, emotional situation, or behavior that brings anxiety.

Secondly, establish an image, voice, or expression to identify the part of yourself the induces the negative mood.

Thirdly, find a positive intent from the situation, perhaps your depression is as a result of a lost car.

Fourthly, respond to the situation by extracting a positive result from the case. You may choose to find and embrace the advantages of walking and using the public transport system.

Fifthly, make sure both parts of your mind, conscious and unconscious, agree. If you find that you are making excuses, then go back to step four.

<u>Anchoring yourself</u>

Anchoring yourself means associating the desired emotional response with a specific sensation and phrase. The analogy of anchoring was deduced from an experiment done on a dog with a ringing bell. The researcher started ringing the bell every eating time. Eventually, the dog connected the ringing bell with food. Each time the bell was rung, even in the absence of food, the dog salivated.

Actually, when you select a positive emotion and intentionally link it to a plain expression, then whenever you feel low you just have to induce this anchor, and there will be a notable and immediate change of the feelings. Achieving the technique is simple:

Firstly, identify the feeling you want to acquire.

Secondly, choose where you want to set the anchor, select an action that you seldom do.

Thirdly, reflect on a past experience that induced the feeling you love and associate to it. As you get the feeling to contact the anchor you choose, maybe by squeezing a particular part of your body

Fourthly, since the anchor has already been established, just trigger it similarly, by yourself.

Fifthly, to enhance the effectiveness of the anchor, recall any other situation that induced your preferred feeling and repeats the above steps.

From there onwards, you can use the technique to induce relaxation and positive feelings.

<u>Mirror</u>

The reflection we have on ourselves portrays our thoughts and perception. However, the mirror technique requires one to insert the feeling that will make people like you. It is considered as the most uncomplicated technique of NLP.

People will only love to assimilate and like people who have confidence in social adaptability. To achieve the technique, observe the body language, way of sitting, and posture of others and assimilate to it calmly and gently. Unconsciously, the person you are likening yourself with will have a different perception on you; in fact, a positive rapport will be created.

Ten ways to protect yourself from Neuro-linguistic Programming

<u>Be extremely wary of people copying your body language</u>

Be genuine and avoid people to copy you. Many NLP adapters will try to copy your style, mode of sitting, how you incline your body, and such things. If you detect such a situation, try to change your style to test the person. When you note the person is copying you, its time you put off your gloves since a cat in gloves catches no mouse.

<u>Move your eyes in random and unpredictable patterns</u>

People who are adapting to NLP will try to copy each bit of your move. They will pay a very close watch to your eyes; as the initial phase of rapport induction. At times you may have a conviction that the people are interested in what you are saying or doing. Surely, they may be, but on the other hand, they are interested in your perception. They carefully watch your eyes to see how you store and retrieve your points and particularly your knowledge. The simple hack for the situation is to randomly move your eyes in a pattern that cannot be easily replicated. This is because, with such actions, they will not be able to detect when you are cooking your words because they cannot identify the part of your brain being used. However, to dodge the clever NLP assimilators, try to make it original by a show of confidence.

<u>Do not let anybody touch you</u>

Whenever you have a close-talk with a friend or a colleague, you may end having an emotional moment. You may just burst into laughter or be in a tear-dropping emotion. If you are aware that the person next to you is into NLP, take a close watch of him/her. If the person touches you sensitively, you should know that he or she is trying to anchor your emotion so that in future he or she can tune you back to that similar emotional state by mere alteration of the trigger. In fact, you should show that, in such a state, the person should not touch you. Otherwise, he or she will gain the power to control your emotions.

<u>Be wary of vague language</u>

According to some established findings, when a language that is not clearly expressed is used, the impact is so high. Use of a vague language is a technique that was developed by Milton Erickson to trigger unconscious condition. The main idea behind the fact is that when a vague language is used, there are high chances that disagreement will be limited. Whenever a clear language is used, it is hard to get into a trance since you are conversant with the kind of presentation. A vague word makes one give in, even though they have no particulate understanding of the same. Can you remember the slogan of Obama during the campaign? Obama used the word 'change' to make his promises and, though many people had less understanding about the word in terms of leadership, they still gave in. That is the power of a vague language, and you should always not fall into the trap.

<u>Be wary of gibberish</u>

Vague language literally applies to the verbal or casual presentation that is not clear to you. On the other hand, a person who is into NLP may use a written work or speech that is incoherent. Gibberish communication is used as an enticement, leading to the phase of NLP. The aim of the tactic is that, the speaker or the writer to tunes your internal emotional state to make you get into what they want you to. However, the structure and meaning of the statement cannot be deduced. To outdo the technique, do not 'understand' what you actually don't. If the language is unclear to you, request for clarification immediately. The statements like 'Please explain your statement, I have not clearly comprehended your wording!' or 'please be more specific about your points!' These statements can break the technique, making it close to useless. It is also a technique that helps you overcome not only the illogical language but also the vague language.

<u>Read between the lines</u>

Have you ever heard a speech or read writing that had less meaning? Actually, it took you time to reread and have repeated listening to try to understand, yet there was no success! That is the reason why to protect yourself from the people who are into NLP you have to read in between the lines. Make sure you leave no stone unturned; interpret each word or component of the speech with keenness. A skilled person, who is into NLP, will formulate a statement that has a top-layered message, but with a hidden and more sensitive message. For example, a person may tell you 'for you to have me you must give me love, yes unstructured love, isn't that good for you and me?' The main point is that he or she needs love from you; however, please note that love should not have conditioned it should be 'unstructured.' You may fall victim in future after things turn bitter and he or she will echo the words 'I said, unstructured love.' To overcome this take time to interpret the sentence bit by bit; otherwise, you will be a win to a person who is into NLP.

<u>Watch your attention</u>

A person who is into NLP can use your attention to overrule you, yes your attention. You should be keen when mingling with people as there are predators who are spying for prey. A person who wants to capture you using your attention, will firstly, make statements that are closely connected to you. At last, he or she will address you directly, mostly, with a question. If you do not read between the lines, you may end up being in agreement that may result in captivity. So to overcome this, make sure you are not only understanding the statement but also try to uncover the intention behind the words regarding your occupation, capabilities, or power. If you are successful in identifying the purpose of the person, then you have invalidated his or her techniques.

<u>Don't agree to anything</u>

We all find ourselves placed in a position that we must make a decision. However, have you ever made a decision that you later wondered how you made it? For example, a person who is in the sales or marketing department may hail the advantages and how good the product is. At the moment, if you are not aware, your emotions are in control of your perception. If you make the decisions so quick, you may end regretting allocating your cash to where you had not planned to. To overcome this frequently used technique from the NLP armed persons, take time to decide. It is also advisable that after you are aware that that particular commodity exists and suits your needs; make a decision of purchase after a while, perhaps after 24 hours. The prolonged time will help you to evaluate the worth, urgency, and friendliness of the commodity. This is of course if, when you were going to a particular place, you had not intended to make the purchase or decision. Perhaps you were going to make a purchase, make sure you have an established stand of particular thing you want and its specifications. Otherwise, you may end up purchasing a commodity that may look similar to the intended one, but different.

You may say 'they cannot convince me,' but note that, most of those salespersons are equipped with NLP techniques and this makes their convictions power more treacherous than professional.

<u>Trust your intuition</u>

The Deities instills a feature that talks to us each time we make a decision; it is called the conscience. Our instincts are manufactured here. Have you have ever intended to do a particular thing but after conviction you quit? The chances are that after the consequences hit hard, you will start to wish you had followed your instincts! Sometimes it is hard or impossible to correct and rectify on the result that is experienced after a given decision.

Our conscience connects us with unknown powers that predict the result of a given decision. Observe sobriety whenever you are making the given decision. As stated earlier, salespersons maybe dodgy leading you to contradict your conscience, which you may remorse about after that. Therefore, make your decision on the basis of your understanding and not convictions.

<u>Be wary of permissive language</u>

How would you feel if you went to purchase a car and the seller commands you to drive test; he or she makes it mandatory? The chances are that you will decline the offer, right? What if, a different person tells you 'hello sir/madam you may take a driving test and confirm that our cars are the best'? The chances are that you will give in. A car seller who is into NLP will use this against you. The permissive language softens your heart and solid-hard decisions. Eventually, you will give in to the convictions. It is wise that you do not give in to the permissive language other it may be leading path to trance.

CHAPTER 9:

Deception Techniques and Overcoming Deceptive Manipulators

Deception is the act of being influenced by your manipulator to get what he or she wants, therefore misleading or promote a specific belief. Fraud is typically done for personal gain and may comprise of dissimulation, distractions, propagandas and concealment statements. Similarly, deception includes self-manipulation when having faith in different subjective implications, bluff, subterfuge, or beguilement. Your manipulator primarily targets emotions resulting in a feeling of distrust and betrayal. With many people expecting friends, relational partners, and even strangers, to be honest, instances of untruthful information are highly to occur.

The current digital world also brings the concern of deception in different formats ranging from violation of specific policies via the internet; hence, the acquisition of reliable information by manipulators. Similarly, other instances include the use of modern devices to detect liars primarily used by the United States government to acquire truth from criminals. Since the introduction of these devices, many victims have obtained justice, therefore, settling complex disagreements. Other terms under deception used by Tue government include misinformation, secrecy, military secrets, and fake news.

Deception in Relationships

Romantic relationships tend to have significant deception practices with an estimate of more than 90% of individuals agreeing to be lying to their partners. Despite not being a continuous behavior, there is a point in time where they are not completely honest. Deception in relationships takes three motivations. First, partner-focus is the situation where a partner lies to prevent any harm, especially emotionally to their partners. Secondly, self-focus entails enhancement or protection of your partner behavior or image in public. And lastly, relationship-focus motives tend to use lies to prevent relationship harm, conflicts, and trauma.

Deception in Religion

Religious discussions also comprise of fraud with several sources try to create a variation between manipulation and religion practices. The topics discussed to highlight how deception is generated in religion, while others insist the sector itself is deceptive lying to followers. For example, the founder of FaithLeaks states that the organization focuses on eliminating facets of untruthfulness and unethical activities witnessed in religion. Christians have been considered critics of deception as well as problematic as well as selfish and bigotry. Subsequently, Islamic Taqiyya concept is said to be decisive while Muslims view it as an alleviated perception in religion.

Deception in Philosophy

Meditation and mind control techniques have been categorized to be decisive, especially in modern philosophy. Numerous arguments emerged to explain how fraud exists in the philosophy that everything we know about the practice may seem wrong and lie. However, different notions used have described varying theories to suggest that the acts of philosophy are free from deception.

Deception in Research

Different studies, especially in psychology, comprises of manipulation, therefore misleading and misinforming the public about its experiments. Some of the deceptive practices involved are acts of lying to participate in research about a scientific study, but in reality, is to learn their behaviors. Deception in psychological research henceforth tricks participants into involving in fake reviews but examiners obtaining different results. The rationale behind deception encompasses the need to lie to their self-consciousness to avoid triggering certain activities which interfere with the intended outcome.

Ways to Defend Against GasLighting

GasLighting is the behavior of a manipulator to influence your mind until you begin questioning your sanity or judgments. The common tactics used include subtle used primarily by narcissistic, abusers, or sociopathic individuals. Such people possess adequate skills to find their way into your mind emotionally, therefore, gaining from your weaknesses. You being a frown up or learned person does not mean that you are free from being manipulated.

Some of the red flags you are susceptible to GasLighting include being uncomfortable when being around them, making your self-control more vulnerable. Other techniques they use are making you feel crazy quickly, responsible for everything; you begin judging yourself and being scared to face them. However, there are several methods to use and defend yourself against GasLighting.

Learn Self-Care Strategies

The first step to prepare from GasLighting is to learn how to protect yourself, especially when you spot manipulators. Self-confidence in facing them they approach enables you to develop on what is coming while standing your boundaries. Listen in on what they say but never give in as their goal is solely to benefit from your immediate kindness. Besides, ensure you remain active and never show pity or become emotional as that is their primary target to weaken your stands.

Avoid Interaction with Manipulators

Some people are incapable of developing firm boundaries with limits; therefore, avoid participating or involving with your manipulator in developing a conversation. Long conversations are among the key elements leading GasLighting, as you may forget all your principles and give in. For instance, you begin the interaction with a lot of energy and capable of standing by your rules. However, when the conversation starts to build up, you may show pity and become emotionally, and that is the beginning of a win for your manipulator.

Confront Them Firmly Without Fear

Another vital step to take is to confront them and let them aware that what they are doing to you or others is not fair at all. Ensure they feel your anger and motive of your points without fear or pity despite their emotional stories. Some of the deceivers maybe your friends, partner, or family member, but remain focused when driving your points. Besides, ensure statements are straightforward without beating around the bush for them to know you are hurt from their activities.

Cut Yourself from Such People

You may have more than one manipulator and probably being your friend or an individual you are well conversant with. Remaining close to such people may at times increase GasLighting events, therefore, benefiting them further over time. Similarly, you may feel reluctant to facing them and letting them know what they are doing is wrong. The best solution hence is to detach yourself from them, reducing the number of meetings within time. Despite the frequent interaction, for instance, avoid conversations that may lead to gossips or acquisition of personal information.

Tips To Protect Yourself against Deception

Deception remains performed in different ways with more techniques emerging hence may become a challenge for you to notice when being deceived. Deception range from traditional method to modern ideas which utilize technology, for example, cybercrime activities. Again, manipulations cases occur across all sectors, including healthcare, government, family, and friends as well as in religion and entrepreneurship. Then, the following are essential tips to consider and protect yourself against deception in the current generation.

Keep Personal Data Secure and Confidential

Manipulators primarily target your personal information, especially through the internet and devices to deceive you until they gain access to your bank or acquire crucial data. As such, the best way to handle such people is to ensure all your vital personal data is kept in a very secure section. The information should as well be challenging for them to acquire despite influencing you the limits. As such, even if you are deceived, you can protect yourself against exposing essential personal data.

Continually Learn Tricks and Warming Signs

When up-to-date with how deceivers use tactics to win their target, ensure you also brush on standard techniques they use. Similarly, learn about some of the warning signs highlighted in the internet, magazines, or advertisements by either victims or researchers. Such activities enable you to remain at the forefront of how to spot and stay away from manipulators. In case a deceiver approaches you and begin his or her influences, you readily notice the sign and able to defend yourself against deception. Besides, ensure you are well equipped to face any difficulties accompanied to prevent falling to unavailable tricks.

Report to Relevant Authorities

Reporting any cyberbullying, scams, or personal manipulation practices also play a significant role in defending yourself against deception. Reporting entails seeking for external assistance to detach yourself from disturbing manipulators. Despite a more substantial percentage of victims going without justice, it enhances your sense of security while facing other emerging manipulators. The same applies to the authority to keep track of such cases, therefore, protecting the general public against deception.

Face Them Openly

Facing a manipulator is one of the crucial elements of ensuring that they never retry deceiving you soon. Confronting manipulators applies to friends, family members, and your spouse or love partner. Drive the instant message of deception using the necessary tone while remaining focused. As mentioned earlier, facing a manipulator make them understand that you not only tolerate their actions but also defending yourself against deception.

Strengthen Your Limit Boundaries

Understanding how manipulators work enables you to figure out some of the tricks used to capitalize on your weaknesses and benefit. Some of these individuals may deceive you naturally, making you end up giving in to their needs. However, when you set healthy boundaries and stand by them, it becomes complicated for them to deceive you quickly. More so, your principles acts are guidelines to ensure you are not vulnerable to deception while preventing you from falling for lies.

Learn Ways out If You Become a Victim

Sometimes a manipulator may overcome all your defenses against deception and gain access to you, making you a victim. Such cases occur, and the best option out is to learn the essential aspects of a way out. Henceforth, learn a few tricks on how to release yourself from the chains of a manipulator who are working to benefit from you. As such, finding your way out acts a crucial mechanism in defending yourself against existing deception practices.

Deception Techniques

As an act of influencing an individual or the public in general, deception takes different techniques to ensure the provision of the intended message effectively. Besides, fraud takes various forms rather than lying. The formats used include equivocation, concealment, exaggeration, untruthful, and understatements. Many manipulators believe that the technique adopted to deceive others is the most effective and unnoticed. However, confidence is frequently misplaced, and they can be easily detected and avoided. Methods of deception henceforth are;

Decoys and Imitation

Imitation is the act of observing and replicating certain behaviors of a person henceforth engaging in social learning. Such impressions create a lure performing a similar task, and its usually not inherited genetically, but another person benefits from your accomplishments. Imitations are sometimes beneficial for different groups, including the transfer of essential information from professionals to beginners. However, the technique can be utilized for certain practices. For instance, soldiers in the 18th century used tree trunks as decoys of a canoe to deceive their enemies.

Concealment

Deception also includes situations where your manipulator omits some information intending to lie as to prevent it from being known. The information provided through concealment may either be a complete lie or the real but eliminating the essential data. As a technique of deception, to conceal, therefore involves lies or hiding of important news leading to the provision of misleading statements. For example, when asked how your day was, you only tell about work but eliminate wrongdoings or daily activities such as lunch and traffic, among others.

Equivocations

Equivocation is the act of using indirect, contradicting, or ambiguous information leading to a false outcome. When explaining a particular incident and using words with more than one meaning, the probability is that there will arise of an event of confusing statements. The technique is not only a lie but a method of deception, creating either a disagreement or vague in misinformation. For example, when someone states, 'cotton is light.' There may exist confusion as 'light' has several meanings; 'bright,' 'start burning' and 'weightlessness.' Therefore, a given group may become deceived about what precisely a manipulator is precisely talking about.

Understatements

Understatement involves minimizing, downplaying, or denying the truth accompanied by rationalizing. The technique is crucial elements, especially when the subject is feeling guilty with words such as minification, belittling, euphemism, and trivializing. Understatements take two forms of manipulation; minimization of misdemeanors when confronted and when denying their victim's positive or negative characteristics. It may also be in the form of cognitive recognition. Besides, understatements include the provision of information with less truth and include literary analogs, depression, and social minimization.

Exaggeration

Exaggeration is the act of providing statements with excessive stress and is usually the opposite of understatement. An exaggerator typically pretends about a particular object, features, or personal qualities to distinguish themselves or meet individual specifications. Some of the expressions usually used are magnification, overreaction, stretching the truth, catastrophization, and hyperbole. As a type of deception, exaggeration entails manipulative people speaking of what would influence you to believe in statements that are never true and misleading.

Simulation

Like imitation, simulation comprises of exhibiting untrue information in three forms; mimicry, distraction, and fabrication. Mimicry is a deceiving nature of showing similarity to other people or objectives. For instance, an animal may mimic a specific behavior to escape from predators or prey. Fabrication involves making a piece of similar equipment to deceive your enemies or allies, for example making of hollow tanks designed from wood as armor in World War II. Distraction, on the other hand, is to seek attention from the truth by using bait or something to evade speaking the truth.

Overcoming Deceptive Manipulators

Know Your Rights

The most significant and vital technique of overcoming a deceptive manipulator is to learn and understand your rights as a human. Knowing your rights enables you to be aware when you are being violated and stand in defense without harming others. The act of spotting and facing a liar without violation of any of your rights, therefore, gives you a great opportunity of overcoming deception. Some of your right to align with are being treated with respect, express feelings and opinions, set priorities, and create a happy and healthy lifestyle.

Ask Probing Questions

A psychological manipulator typically goes ahead, making demands or requests making you feel responsible and volunteer to help them. As an individual, it is, however, useful to begin asking probing questions by changing the focus to them. Probing questions trigger their guilt, making you understand their self-awareness henceforth recognizing the inequalities they are creating. Besides, it enables the manipulator to see their motive of their requests or demands, leading to a loose of his or her side.

Take Time to Respond To Their Requests and Demands

Manipulators understand how they work; as such, they primarily rely on your immediate answer as to make their next move. As to overcome such trick, utilize time to isolate yourself from them by asking for more time and think about their requests or demands. Again, taking sometimes makes you weigh the benefits against detriments and decide what to do at the end. Time is thus an influential factor in overcoming a deceptive manipulator.

Say No Occasionally but Firmly

Learning to Say 'no' firmly is one of the arts of communication skills used to speak to someone diplomatically. With strong boundary principles and well prepared to face your manipulator, you are quickly destined to provide an authoritative 'no' answer to their demands. Your firm 'no' response should accompany forms such as determine and assert consequences. Such results are suitable for sophisticated deceptive manipulators who are hard to take 'no' as an answer to their continual deception techniques.

Conclusion

Thank you for making it through to the end *How to Analyze People*. I hope this book has been an informative and practical journey for you and that it serves you well in your personal and professional life. You've been provided with all of the tools you need to achieve your goals whatever they may be. The world is your playground. If you put your imagination to it, there is an opportunity in every single interaction you have, if you look for it.

Finally, if you found this book useful in any way, a review on Amazon is always appreciated!